# Cinema Is a Cat

## A Cat Lover's Introduction to Film Studies

Daisuke Miyao

University of Hawai'i Press
Honolulu

24  23  22  21  20  19          6  5  4  3  2  1

**Library of Congress Cataloging-in-Publication Data**

Names: Miyao, Daisuke, author. | Miyao, Daisuke. Eiga wa neko de aru.
Title: Cinema is a cat : a cat lover's introduction to film studies /
    Daisuke Miyao.
Description: Honolulu : University of Hawai'i Press, 2019. | Loosely based
    on the author's Eiga wa neko de aru, Tokyo, 2011. | Includes
    bibliographical references and index.
Identifiers: LCCN 2019021389 | ISBN 9780824879709 (paperback) | ISBN
    9780824879693 (cloth)
Subjects: LCSH: Cats in motion pictures. | Motion pictures. |
    Cinematography.
Classification: LCC PN1995.9.A5 M59 2019 | DDC 791.43/629752—dc23
LC record available at https://lccn.loc.gov/2019021389

University of Hawai'i Press books are printed on acid-free
paper and meet the guidelines for permanence and
durability of the Council on Library Resources.

# Cinema Is a Cat

In memory of Charles Silver, a lover of cats and cinema

# Contents

# Acknowledgments

I am deeply indebted to the unchanging enthusiasm, encouragement, and generosity of my editor at the University of Hawai'i Press, Pamela Kelley, who helped make this book possible. She meticulously read my manuscript and made a number of insightful and caring comments and suggestions.

I would like to thank two anonymous readers at the University of Hawai'i Press for their valuable suggestions. I also want to thank Jennifer McIntyre for scrupulously and gracefully copyediting my manuscript.

Special thanks go to Shibata Motoyuki and Mari Yoshihara, who read the first draft of the Japanese edition of *Cinema Is a Cat;* Markus Nornes, who first suggested that I write an English edition; Matsui Jun and Mizuno Yoshimi of Heibonsha, who published the Japanese edition in 2011 and supported the publication of this English edition as well; Marianne McDonald, Cristina Della Coletta, and Yingjin Zhang of UCSD, who have provided generous institutional support; Larry McCallister of Paramount Pictures Theatrical Library; Paul G. Alberghetti and Michael O. Crain of the Audrey Hepburn Estate, who have given permission to use the photograph of Audrey Hepburn and a cat for the book cover.

A very early version of chapter five appeared in *The Journal of Japanese and Korean Cinema* 8.2 (2016) with support from the editors of the journal, Hye Seung Chung and David Scott Diffrient.

To Yoko, Dica (who has crossed over the Rainbow Bridge), Dot, and Hoku, the loves of my life, I am truly grateful for the happiness that you have brought to us. I could not even think of writing this book or the Japanese edition without you.

Last of all but equally importantly, I would like to express my deepest gratitude to the humane societies and the rescue groups around the globe. Thank you so much for the brave and selfless work you do on behalf of those who cannot advocate for themselves.

# Cinema Is a Cat

"... should you wish to learn about cats, only a cat can tell you."

—Natsume Sōseki, *I Am a Cat*

The nameless cat of Japanese author Natsume Sōseki's acclaimed 1905 novel laments that cats are beyond human comprehension. The cat is absolutely right. Even for a cat lover like me, cats are like phantoms. I know my cats like small, dark places. I have seen that they enjoy watching and chasing, and I consider them to be good performers and fussy eaters. To be honest, though, I still don't understand how they think and what they really like. But I am very attracted to them.

I am also a cinephile. To me, cinema is like a cat. Until very recently, cinema has existed in (relatively) small and dark places called movie theaters. It is something to be watched and enjoyed visually. Many films are about the chase, and of course acting is an integral part of cinema. Screening schedules are usually rigid, as firm as mealtimes. I have been watching cinema for more than forty years and have been studying it for more than twenty-five. I have read a book by André Bazin, an influential French film critic, entitled *What is Cinema?*, but to be frank, I still don't know how to define it. Yet I am strongly attracted to cinema.

Film scholar Rey Chow calls cinema "phantomlike" (Chow 2001, 1391). In her essay that surveys the history of the academic study of cinema, Chow suggests that cinema will remain an "ambiguous" object of study because both teachers of the humanities and amateur film lovers without formal training contribute to knowledge production around it (Chow 2001, 1391–1392). But in such phantomlike ambiguity, concludes Chow, "may lie its most interesting intellectual future" (Chow 2001, 1392).

In this book, I hunt for the phantoms. I pursue the "interesting intellectual future" of cinema using the cat, a "phantomlike" being, as a guide. I admit this is an arbitrary and very personal choice. I am doing this because cats and cinema have had tremendous influences on my life during the last two decades. I was born and raised in Japan. When I first came to the United States in the mid-1990s to study cinema in New York, I became friends with a cat who belonged to my future partner. She had adopted the cat, which she named Dica, from a rescue organization, and the three of us watched films together in our apartment in Brooklyn (we only had a very small TV, not even digital, and a VHS deck). After several years I found a job teaching film at a university on the West Coast, and we three crossed America together. The cat died in 2008, and I wrote a Japanese forerunner to this book, *Cinema Is a Cat (Eiga wa neko dearu)*, soon afterwards. When the book was eventually published in 2011, it seemed like my requiem to our beloved cat.

Dudley Andrew, a film scholar whom I deeply admire, wrote, "Every genuine cinematic experience involves *décalage,* time-lag" (Andrew 2009, 914). Unlike later media, including TV and the internet, which strive for immediacy, cinema exists in "a gap between here and there as well as now and then" (Andrew 2009, 914). The film image that we see now is always the one filmed and edited in the past. Filmmakers and spectators are separated by time and space. Andrew concluded that "perhaps it took later media—and particularly the new media of video games, the interactive internet, and virtual reality —to let us recognize that cinema has never really been about immediacy. Its spontaneity and contingency—its neorealism—has always been the lure by which it offers an experience that, properly speaking, is not immediate at all, but reflective, resonant, and voluminous" (Andrew 2009, 915). Perhaps it took the death of my cat to make me realize how important she had been in my life. I had taken her existence for granted when she was alive. My genuine experience of my cat can now exist only in "*décalage,* time-lag." When I wrote my Japanese-language book about cats and cinema, it was the first time I had seriously thought about the fact that cinema can only exist in time-lag.

This English-language book, *Cinema Is a Cat,* is loosely based on the 2011 Japanese version. It is about cinema, which is "reflective, resonant, and voluminous" in nature, a point that is especially important to remember now when a number of people in both the entertainment and academic worlds, facing the dominance of new media, address the "death of cinema."

Acclaimed filmmakers such as Martin Scorsese and Ridley Scott have charged that filmmakers have become overly reliant on digital techniques and computer-generated images, that the industry has become risk averse and franchise obsessed. They lament that cinema has become more television-like, more game-like, and that moviegoing is no longer a community-building activity. To them, the cinema that they love is dying. Scholars, too, facing the shift from celluloid to digital filmmaking and from moviegoing to social networking, have had to adapt. The academic field of film studies has morphed into media studies and cultural studies. For some scholars, the celluloid cinema has become an archeological object.

Still, I don't think this book is an archaic project facing only toward the past. Indeed, in this world of new media, our lives are surrounded by moving images: television, video, YouTube, streaming, GPS, virtual reality. As long as our moving image culture continues, cinema will always be shown somewhere, somehow; therefore, the practical and theoretical study of cinema by filmmakers and critics/scholars/cinephiles will not disappear. The methodological and philosophical endeavor to define what cinema is will continue, along with a new question: What are these new media? Thus, the legacy of film studies—how to read audiovisual materials aesthetically and culturally—has a limitless value for the future. I hope this book will be an introduction both to that legacy and to the expanding universe of film studies. After all, the field of film studies has been expanding since the 1950s, when literature teachers first started offering film analysis in their courses. And over the years, other disciplines including art history, sociology, anthropology, history, psychology, and economics have recognized cinema's attractions (Andrew 2009, 882–883).

This book is also about cats. A major difference between the Japanese and English versions of *Cinema Is a Cat* is that this one faces firmly toward the future. The English edition is not a simple translation of the Japanese one. It contains brand-new chapters and this new prologue. All other chapters have been substantially reimagined and rewritten for new readers. While the Japanese book was written in memory of my deceased cat, I am writing this book with two new cats at my side. We watch films together every night.

In the chapters that follow, I make a number of connections between cats and cinema. One reason for this is that cats have played important roles in the history of cinema. There are four historically significant films that all have close connections to cats. One of them is *Avatar* (James Cameron, 2009), the highest-grossing film of all time. Cats inspired the creators of the aliens in this film, and the cute, feline-like appearance of the aliens helps strengthen the audience's emotional attachment to them.

Another is *The Third Man* (Carol Reed, 1949), considered the best British film of the twentieth century by the British Film Institute in 1999 and the best film of all time by *Kinema Junpō,* the most influential film magazine in Japan. In the film Harry Lime (Orson Welles), who has been in hiding, is forced to make his first appearance in the film when his cat draws close to him, exposing his presence.

In *The Godfather* (Francis Ford Coppola, 1972), the second-best film in the American Film Institute's *100 Years . . . 100 Films* list (2007), the tough gangster Don Corleone (Marlon Brando) holds a cat in his arms while petting him very gently. His act is a stark contrast to the brutality that he shows on different occasions even as it mirrors the affection he shows his loved ones. (It is said that Brando, a cat lover, found the stray cat on the set and worked it into the scene).

Finally, one of the oldest films in the world, a thirty-second film produced by Thomas Edison, the king of inventors, in 1894, is entitled *The Boxing Cats.* In the film, two cats wear boxing gloves and fight in a tiny ring. Behind them is "Prof. Welton," who smiles and lets them fight on (a cruel act, from a cat lover's point of view).

The Lumière brothers (Auguste and Louis), Edison's rivals, whose first paid public screening of their films on December 26, 1895, is considered by many to be the beginning of cinema, also produced at least seven films with cats between 1896 and 1900.

Today in the new media landscape, cat videos are a major genre of popular Web culture. One star in particular was born from the genre: Maru, a Scottish Fold cat. As of September 2016, videos featuring Maru had been viewed over 325 million times. The appeal of the cat in visual media has been strong and enduring.

Another reason why I've chosen to highlight cats in cinema is that there are similar characteristics between these two "phantomlike" subjects. By directing your attention to the fascinating relationships between cats and cinema, I offer a unique and intimate view of the history and theories of cinema. Cats are major representational subjects in the nine films explored in this book (nine because people say cats have nine lives), and in each chapter, I juxtapose a feline characteristic—"Cats love small spaces" or "Cats love dark places"—with discussion of the languages, theories, and history of cinema.

In Part I, I focus on three basic elements of the language of cinema: framing, lighting, and editing. It was Yoshimura Kōzaburō, the acclaimed Japanese director of *The Ball at the Anjo House* (*Anjō ke no butōkai,* 1947) starring Hara Setsuko, who selected *Cinema Is a Frame!* (*Eiga wa furēmu da!*) to be the title of his 2001 book. *Painting with Light* is the title of a 1995 book on cinematography by John Alton, who received an Oscar for *An American in Paris* (Vincente Minnelli, 1951). Francis Ford Coppola of *The Godfather* is often quoted as saying, "The essence of cinema is editing." I illuminate these three essential functions of film by invoking three well-known passions of cats: small spaces, dark places, and the chase.

My emphasis in these first three chapters is on close analysis of the audiovisual text of cinema, and I introduce some of the "bedrock information" of how to read the cinematic text (Andrew 2009, 905). In the US, it has been predominantly film scholar David Bordwell who has addressed the importance of close analysis in order to establish film studies as an academic discipline. To do so, Bordwell has chosen to pay "attention to the specific and systematic character of the medium" (Andrew 2009, 902). In Japan, it has been Hasumi Shigehiko who has similarly focused on close analysis. Using the term "surface criticism" ("*hyōsō hihyō*"), Hasumi emphasized the significance of paying attention to the details of techniques in order to distinguish film studies from literary criticism or journalistic reviews (Hasumi 1990, 180–214). My arguments in these three chapters are inspired by Bordwell and Hasumi.

After introducing the analytical methods in the first three chapters, we move on to the contexts in which films are made, exhibited, and viewed by turning to the theory and history of cinema. In the chapters that follow, paying attention to the language of cinema that we have learned in Part I, I introduce the major theoretical and methodological concepts of film studies that have developed first in France and England, and then in the United States over the fifty years following World War II. The concepts are as follows: auteurism, realism, genre, feminist film theory, stardom, national cinema, and modernity theory.

Auteurism, realism, and genre can be attributed to the French film critics of the journal *Cahiers du cinéma* in the 1950s. Auteurist critics began to closely analyze the visual styles of cinema in order to distinguish cinema from literature or screenplays. Those critics considered filmmakers who impart their own styles to their films, regardless of the genre, to be auteurs. Auteurs, according to those critics, were conscious of the movie camera's capability of mechanical reproduction, which is what separates cinematic realism from painting and even from photography.

Later, with the emergence and flourishing of feminist film theory in 1970s England, a psychoanalytic essay, "Visual Pleasure and Narrative Cinema," by Laura Mulvey, became influential. Her essay shifted the focus of film studies from analysis of the film form to that of the film viewing experience. In particular, she attacked mainstream cinema for the way it turned female characters into objects of the desiring male gaze. Star studies developed along with feminist film theory and paid particular attention to Marxist analysis, in which a star is seen not so much as an individual but as an image or commodity.

Then, in the "explosion of American film studies" since the 1980s (Andrew 2009, 900), attention has turned to cultural studies of film production and reception, focusing on issues of racism, nationalism, colonialism, and historical specificity, including modernity and modernization.

Thus in Part II, we make use of the methods and theories of film studies, asking questions such as: Who is the author of a film? How does a film connect to reality? What connections does one film have to other films? Who is represented in a film and how? How is a film produced and viewed differently by people with different cultural and social backgrounds? How is a film located in history? Our focus on the innate behaviors of cats offers what I hope will be a memorable and appealing approach to these questions. There are, of course, many more technical, theoretical, and historical issues in film studies than what I deal with in this book. It would be my great pleasure if you, whether a cat lover, a film lover, or both, become interested in film studies after reading this book and find new ways to enjoy watching and talking about cinema . . . and cats.

## Author's note:

In this book, translations from Japanese-language books are my own unless otherwise noted. Japanese names are listed family name first, except for the ones that are commonly used in English (e.g., Sessue Hayakawa). Macrons/diacritics are not used in English translations of Japanese titles: *The Period that Toyo Miyatake Looked into (Tōyō Miyatake ga nozoita jidai*, 2008).

## Note:

*Epigraph.* Natsume Sōseki, *I Am a Cat* (1905, 2001; 19)

# PART I

# The Languages of Cinema

# CHAPTER 1

# Cats Love Small Spaces

### Framing in *Breakfast at Tiffany's*

*Blake Edwards, USA, 1961*

## Having Breakfast at Tiffany's

Fifth Avenue, Manhattan. Early in the morning. The city is quiet. A taxi slides onto the screen from afar, where we see the Empire State Building in the distance. The soft melody of "Moon River" by Henry Mancini begins. The taxi stops in front of 727 Fifth Avenue. A slender woman in a black dress, long gloves, and black sunglasses, carrying a brown paper bag, gets out and looks up at the name on the building: Tiffany & Co. The clock under the name shows five forty-five. When she walks toward a show window, the credit appears right next to her slender body: Audrey Hepburn.

Standing in front of the show window, where expensive jewelry is displayed, Hepburn opens the brown bag and takes out a paper cup of coffee

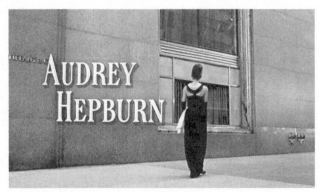

Holly Golightly (Audrey Hepburn) stands in front of Tiffany & Co.

Holly is captured in the glass window.

and a pastry. She bites off a small piece of pastry, sips coffee, and moves to the next window. She is vaguely reflected in the glass. The following shot shows Hepburn's face from inside the building, as seen through the glass window. Hepburn's face is so perfectly framed by the window that she herself looks like a beautiful mannequin with expensive jewelry, sunglasses, and a Givenchy dress. Critic Rachel Mosley writes that for Marilyn Monroe, clothes were about showing off her body, but for Hepburn the reverse was true: her body was for showing off the clothes (Mosley 2002, 179).

Then, the camera moves outside again. Hepburn slowly starts walking north on Fifth Avenue and turns right onto 57th Street. She tosses the breakfast that she has barely touched into a trash bin. The moon is no longer in the sky, but she walks in the direction of the East River to the melody of "Moon River." The morning sunlight is faint, and she casts almost no shadow on the street. Hepburn's steps are slow but look very light because of that. In fact, the name of the character that Hepburn plays in this film is Holly Golightly. Holly goes lightly. In the original novel by Truman Capote, Holly's mailbox reads, "Holly Golightly: Traveling." Is traveling her occupation, or is she on a trip? In fact, Holly is a high-class call girl. She must be on her way back from work. She never takes off her sunglasses. She may want to hide rings under her eyes. But her steps and behavior are so light, almost casual, that it looks as if she happened to wake up early and come out for a walk in a deserted city with her breakfast. Just as a cat takes a walk early in the morning.

According to Iwagō Mitsuaki, a popular animal photographer in Japan, early morning is the best time to meet cats in any town and photograph them. Many cat owners experience their cats waking up quite early, climbing up on the bed, kneading the blanket, tapping on their face with their paws, and requesting breakfast. Iwagō writes, "The beauty of cats in the morning light is particularly noteworthy. So every moment in the morning is precious for me to meet as many beautiful cats as possible" (Iwagō 2007, 23). Early morning seems to be the best time to meet Holly in the city, too.

## Holly Behaves Like a Cat

This is how *Breakfast at Tiffany's,* a sophisticated urban romantic comedy starring Audrey Hepburn, begins. As this opening scene implies, Holly is depicted throughout this film as if she were a cat. First of all, many of her actions and behaviors remind us of a cat. While Holly scornfully calls the men she dates for work "rats," her job is to make "trips to the powder room" for them. She cannot live without putting powder on her face, dressing up in Givenchy dresses, going to parties, and hunting those rats. Holly says she has dined with (as opposed to "upon," one might surmise!) twenty-seven rats in only two months. In order to emphasize the "rat"-ness of her customers, or their lack of high moral status, most men in this film are shorter than the women. For instance, in a party scene at Holly's apartment, Hollywood producer OJ (Martin Balsam) takes a girl named Irving into a bathroom. Yet, Irving is much taller than OJ, so it looks as though it is she who takes him. Irving is most likely another call girl. She has probably caught a rat that evening.

In addition to her early morning walk and her job hunting rats, Holly behaves like a cat in other ways. After her breakfast at Tiffany's, she goes back to her brownstone apartment building on the Upper East Side (East 71st Street, to be exact). She runs up the steps of her building as if she were running away from the sunlight, which has suddenly become stronger. Once inside, she lightly climbs the stairs after asking Yuniyoshi, the building's Japanese super, to unlock the door. Yuniyoshi, played by Mickey Rooney, horribly made up with lifted eyes, round black glasses, and protruding teeth, loudly complains because Holly always forgets her key and bothers him, relentless as a cat. And just as cats like to climb, Holly goes up and down stairs many times in this film, including the staircases of the apartment and the emergency stairs outside her window.

In her apartment, Holly often uses a kitchen drawer as a step and climbs up on the counter to reach for a liquor bottle at the top of a cupboard. She sits on the counter with her legs sticking into the kitchen sink. This cupboard and the sink are the favorite places of Holly's cat as well. The cat is called Cat because it does not have a name. When Holly comes home, Cat

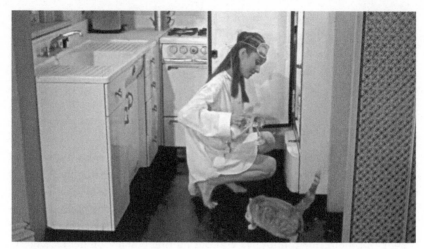

Holly and her cat, Cat.

usually waits for her in the sink. When Holly has a party in her apartment, the cat escapes to the top of the cupboard. The favorite drink of Cat and Holly appears to be milk. At night, Holly drinks a cocktail in a martini glass. Is it a glass of Kahlua and milk, a white Russian? In the morning, she sleepily opens her refrigerator and has milk in a martini glass. Holly gives the same milk to her nameless cat. (In reality, however, many cats are lactose intolerant and allergic to milk.)

Cat is a so-called shoulder cat and particularly likes to perch on the shoulders of men. When the young author Paul, who will fall in love with Holly, visits her apartment for the first time, Cat jumps up on his shoulder right away. Cat climbs on another man's shoulder during Holly's party—and so, surprisingly, does Holly. In fact, she climbs onto men's shoulders quite often. For example, when she sees her husband, Doc Golightly (Buddy Ebsen), a veterinarian whom she married in Texas when she was thirteen, after many years, this strong man of the West picks her up and carries her on his shoulders. It is veterinarians who save and protect animals, and likewise, young Holly may have been protected by the veterinarian as if she were a cat.

## Is Holly Free? Are Cats Free?

Holly's behaviors are not the only thing that connects her to cats; they also share similar living conditions. Holly insists that she is a "free spirit." She is a "wild thing" and will not succumb to men, including Doc Golightly. Holly's insistence on being a "free spirit" anticipates the cultural upheaval of the

1960s when freedom was invoked in matters of race, sex, and politics all over the world. Cats, too, have long been a symbol of freedom and independence in cultures around the globe. Many a cat owner has felt a little lonesome when their cat does not react as they hope, especially when they call their names or try to play with them.

Still, the equation of cats and freedom may be overly simplistic. In fact, as early as 3,500 BC, wild cats were domesticated and turned into pets in Egypt. Egyptian farmers needed them to hunt the rats and moles that ruined their fields. A Chinese character for cat is a combination of an animal and a seedling. In both cultures, cats that fulfilled this role were provided with a safe home and sufficient food. Thus, cats have been kept and enclosed by humans for a long time. They have been far from free or wild in any true sense.

In this film, Holly's nameless cat cannot go outside. Just as the cat is confined in the apartment, Holly in this film is depicted as a captive, especially by way of framing. There is always a square frame in cinema. It is the space enclosed by the frame of a camera. The shot can be close-up (camera tightly frames an object or a human face), medium shot (or waist shot), long shot (typically shows the entire object or human body), high-angle (camera looks down), or low-angle (camera looks up). The aspect ratio between the width and height of the frame can be 1.33: 1 (standard), 1.85: 1 (widescreen)—like this film—or 2.66: 1 (CinemaScope). The camera can move or zoom. Yet, the square frame always exists. *Breakfast at Tiffany's* uses the square frame effectively and expressively to emphasize the sense of confinement around Holly.

For instance, Holly is often caught between the two doors at the entrance of her apartment building because she keeps losing or forgetting her keys. On those occasions, the camera captures Holly from the ceiling (a high-angle shot), and frames her within a very tiny space surrounded by

Holly is surrounded by handrails.

two walls and two doors. She looks exactly like a prisoner. After she enters the building, Holly often stands behind the staircase banisters, looking as if she were in a cage. To Yuniyoshi, who lives on the top floor, Holly looks surrounded by the numerous handrails.

Moreover, on many occasions Holly fits into square frames within the camera frame itself, such as window frames, glass show windows, and mirrors (for example, a mirror stand in her room, a bathroom mirror, the mirror of a powder compact; even her mailbox has a tiny mirror). It is as if she were imprisoned by frames.

Further strengthening the theme of imprisonment, even though Holly herself is not serving time or under probation, she must travel to Sing Sing Prison by train from Grand Central every Thursday, where she visits an Italian mafia boss. In the end, the police discover that the don has been using her as a courier: she has been a messenger of the crime syndicate without knowing

Holly framed in a mirror.

Holly still looks like a prisoner.

Paul also looks like a prisoner.

it. She is arrested, handcuffed, and locked in jail. The following morning when she is released, her figure is shown "through the barred windows" (Lehman and Luhr 1981, 62). As such, even when she exits the jail, it looks as if she were still a prisoner.

Curiously, it is not only Holly who is depicted in this film as a captive. So is the other protagonist of this film, Paul Varjak (George Peppard), who calls himself a writer. Paul lives his life being "kept" by a rich married woman dubbed 2E (Patricia Neal). In a scene in which 2E receives Paul's phone call in her luxurious apartment, she sits on a comfortable-looking sofa and gently pets a dog by her side, almost as if she were caressing Paul. While Holly is like a cat, Paul is like a dog, faithful to its owner; like Holly, he is also confined into a small space. When 2E looks up at Paul's window, a low-angle shot shows him standing inside the window as if he were a prisoner and not allowed to go outside without her permission.

## When the Two Prisoners Meet: The Framed World

There are two particular scenes in which the framing effectively emphasizes the enclosed situations of the two, like a cat and a dog: the first is when Holly meets Paul for the first time, and the second is when they spend their first night together. The framing in these scenes also underscores the strong bond that forms between the two protagonists.

The first scene takes place when Paul moves into the apartment building where Holly lives. Holly opens her door slightly and looks out into the corridor. In a close-up, Holly's face is caught in a slight space between the door and the wall. This white door also has numerous vertical lines on it, giving her the appearance of an animal looking out from its cage. Similarly, in a medium shot, Paul stands behind the handrails of the staircase looking as if he, too, were behind the bars of a different cage. The shot reverse shot technique, where one character is shown looking at another character and then the other character is shown looking back at the first character, is used here between Holly's face (in a close-up) and Paul standing on the staircase (in a medium shot). The framing of these shots places each character in their own cage and makes it look as though there is a great distance between the two. In addition, Holly wears the earplugs she sleeps with, so there is a sound barrier between them in addition to the visual barriers.

After some exchanges of words that do not make sense, Holly takes out her earplugs. When the camera captures Holly at a closer distance within its frame (in other words, in an extreme close-up), those vertical lines almost disappear from the screen. In a close-up of Paul's face that follows,

Paul is caged behind the handrails.

Holly is caught between the door and the wall.

Close-up of Holly.

Close-up of Paul.

the handrail "bars" vanish, too. As such, the audio and visual cages that have separated them disappear. The framing used for these shots visually shows that the two main characters are making a psychological and emotional connection.

Unfortunately, reality brings them back to their confined situations. It is Thursday morning, and Holly has to hurry to Sing Sing. Cat-like, Holly jumps over her sofa and runs to her bathroom. She brushes her teeth in front of a Japanese-style screen, which also resembles a lattice cage. A bathroom mirror, a mirror stand, and the mirror on the mailbox appear one after another and capture Holly within their square frames over and over again. Finally, Holly crawls under the bed like a cat and fishes out a pair of high heels—called "kitten heels" in the 1960s. Wearing kitten heels was considered to be a first step to adulthood for girls. But the height of the kitten heels still restricts Holly's action.

## The 180-Degree Rule in Hollywood Cinema

In the second example, the scene in which Holly and Paul spend the night together for the first time, framing plays an important role once again in order to emphasize the situations of the two prisoners. One evening, in the middle of a party in her apartment, Holly cannot help running away from the chaos created by her "rats." Seen from outside the building, Holly looks doubly captured by the window frames and by the dark handrails of the emergency staircase.

Holly manages to get out of a window, goes up one floor using the emergency staircase, and peeks into Paul's room. A close-up shot shows only the top half of Holly's face in the window frame. Here again, she looks like a cat peering out of a hiding place. Holly's eyes are shining and look as curious as those of a cat.

The following long shot frames Holly's face in front and Paul and 2E in a bright room at the back—a composition with depth. Such framing further emphasizes Holly's cat-like behavior, hiding in a dark emergency staircase and sneaking a look inside where Paul is sleeping in his bed; he is tightly confined in a window frame in the shot.

After 2E leaves the room, Holly opens the window slightly and continues to look at Paul. A white curtain with numerous vertical lines, hung beside the window, makes another cage for her. Paul jumps up, surprised at Holly's sudden intrusion, but covers himself in the sheets because he is only wearing underwear. Thus, he is also figuratively "tied" to the bed for the sake of decency. Smoothly jumping into the room from the window, just like a cat, Holly enters Paul's room for the first time. She then walks around restlessly, again just like a cat. Cats are nervous when they are in an unfamiliar space and must sneak around and investigate their surroundings first before calming down. Holly lightly sits down on a chair, stretches out her arms and leans on a table, again like a cat. But she stands up right away and pours some liquor (not milk) into a glass that she will never drink. Trying to keep Holly at the center of the frame of long shots, the camera keeps moving gradually from right to left and from front to back. Holly then finds Paul's book, *Nine Lives,* a reference to the expression, "A cat has nine lives," at the back of the room. In Truman Capote's original novel, Paul is yet to publish a book, and there is no *Nine Lives.* In the film, Paul's completed book has been added in order to emphasize the role of cats in it. At this point, Holly finally sits lightly on a chair. She leans on a table, again like a cat, and speaks to Paul.

Suddenly, as film historians Peter Lehman and William Luhr point out, a shot taken from the opposite side of the room is inserted (Lehman and Luhr 1981, 65). Up to this point, ever since Holly came into Paul's room, all shots have been taken from the side where Paul's bed is. In contrast, the shot that appears now is taken from the window from which Holly entered—from 180 degrees opposite. Before this shot, when Paul and Holly are seen together within a frame, he is in the bed in the right front and she is near the window at the back left. Now they are abruptly framed from a completely opposite direction: Holly is now in the right front and Paul is in his bed at the back left.

In Hollywood cinema, there is a technique of framing and editing called the 180-degree rule. (We will discuss editing further in chapter three.) According to this rule, the initial shot of a scene draws an imaginary line, called the axis of action, which divides the action space into two halves. The first one is where the camera is located, while the second one is on the other side of that line. This setup allows the camera position to be varied between

Paul is in the bed in the right front, and Holly stands near the window at the back left.

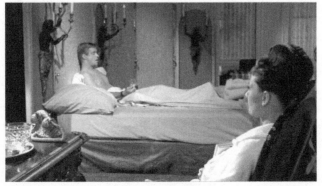

Violation of Hollywood's 180-degree system.

shots, as long as the centerline is not crossed. Once a camera is placed, it must stay on the same side of that line and cannot cross the axis of action in the scene. For example, in this scene of Holly and Paul's conversation, once the camera is set at the side of Paul's bed, it cannot cross the 180-degree line between Holly and Paul. Yet, it does.

The 180-degree system is a general rule in Hollywood cinema not to be broken. In this scene, however, the rule is broken and the couple are photographed from the opposite side. As a result, it may look to the viewers that they have moved and switched their positions. If the viewers are perplexed like this even for a moment, then they may come to their senses instead of remaining absorbed in the story of Holly and Paul. In order to avoid such confusion and a disruption from the storyline, Hollywood filmmakers need to follow a number of rules, including this 180-degree system.

There must be a special reason, then, behind the adoption of the reversed framing here that breaks the golden rule. In this scene, Holly freely moves around like a cat, while Paul is stuck in bed. They apparently have two different characteristics. The reversed framing and the violation of the 180-degree rule may imply that they are actually in the same situation. By positioning the two actors in the same places in the "new" camera frames, the compilation of these shots indicates that they are both prisoners. Even if there is a risk that we the viewers may feel awkward for a moment, the director, the producer, or the cinematographer probably thought it important to indicate the similarity between the two characters.

After this one shot, the camera goes back to its original position and never again crosses the 180-degree line. It is as though the breaking of the rules makes the point, and then things go back to normal, underscoring visually the common conditions that Holly and Paul are under.

After this brief but imposing framing is inserted, Holly resumes her wandering around the room, and the confined situation that she and Paul share becomes more and more visible. When the camera moves and follows Holly in a long shot, we notice that there is another room in front of Paul's bed. A beaded curtain separates the two rooms. The curtain creates a number of vertical lines within the frame, which makes it appear that Holly and Paul are in jail. Holly then opens the curtain and comes into the room in front. She stands in front of a mirror on the left wall and throws the amber liquor from the glass into a flowerpot. (She probably does not like it because the drink is not a milky color.) She is captured in a mirror again. But if we look closely, it is not only Holly who is caught in the mirror: Paul is also reflected in the mirror behind her. The two are now caught together. Holly goes back to the room behind the curtain and sits on the bed where Paul is.

The following shot of the two does not show the mirror or the bead curtain any longer. Instead, for the first time, their bodies touch. Holly slips into the bed and draws close to Paul's naked chest in a closer shot (a medium shot). The barriers between them appear to have vanished. Still, the sense of being caught remains, this time because of content regulations. Under the Production Code, the Hollywood film industry's self-regulation of films' content, which was first enforced in 1934, films could not show sexual relationships between unmarried couples because premarital sex was considered immoral. Showing nudity, either male or female, was not banned, but was nonetheless severely controlled as well.

Here, Holly says, "We're friends. That's all," to Paul, to herself, and to us the viewers, and falls asleep right away. The couple spends their first night together in one bed in the same frame, but under very regulated conditions.

## Escape from the Framed World

The two prisoners continue to attempt to escape from their situations. As we have seen, the enclosed conditions of Holly and Paul are expressed by framing in conspicuous ways. Now the color scheme within the frames starts to play an important role to highlight their escape attempts.

Holly's framed world has been monotonous until Paul appears. In Holly's apartment, both the bedroom and the kitchen are all white. Holly and Cat sip white milk. Her pajamas, a man's tuxedo shirt, are white. When she visits Paul's apartment from the emergency exit, Holly puts on a white bathrobe. Her dress, gloves, and sunglasses when she has breakfast at Tiffany's are all black. On Thursday morning, she wears a black dress, wide hat, and kitten heels to visit Sing Sing. At the Port Authority, she puts on a white scarf when she sees off Doc Golightly. When she becomes drunk at the strip club that evening, she is in a black shirt with black sunglasses and drinks a white cocktail.

Paul is depicted as a person who brings color to Holly's black-and-white world. When he enters Holly's apartment for the first time, color suddenly appears in the monotone space within the frames. As Paul stands beside a shelf, we see for the first time that colorful photographs have been casually placed on it. Holly invites him into the living room and sits on a sofa that we haven't seen before, decorated with red and purple cushions. Then, when Holly impatiently prepares for her visit to Sing Sing, she asks Paul to look for her shoes. He moves to her bedroom and sits on a vivid red blanket. When Holly becomes drunk and Paul brings her back on his shoulder, they are framed under a soft pink light. The light probably comes from the neon sign outside, but it looks as if Paul has brought a warm color to her room.

When Paul receives a check from his publisher, he takes Holly out, saying, "We'll spend the day doing things we've never done before." The scene that follows is the most colorful in the whole film. Almost all shots have bright colors in their frames.

First, Holly seems to be naked when she sees Paul at the door. After inviting him in, she says, "Would you turn around for a second?" and puts on a vivid orange robe. After giving canned food to her cat (the cat looks happy because this is the very first time that we see it being fed in the film), they go out. Holly wears an orange coat that is as vivid as the robe. In a long shot, the two wait for the traffic signal hand in hand, and we see the blue sky behind them. Thanks to the blue sky, the confined nature of the camera frame seems expanded around them. In other words, the couple appears to be in a wide open space for the very first time. The "Don't Walk" sign changes to "Walk," and it looks as though their escape from the framed world has begun.

The couple is headed to Tiffany's, Holly's dream place. As they push open the revolving door to enter, the big store with its high ceilings welcomes them. The extreme long shot of the interior of Tiffany's emphasizes the openness of the space.

In the following shot, their figures are reflected in a mirror on the wall and appear to be captured in a frame momentarily, but a clerk approaches them quickly. As they move to the right, the camera follows. As a result, the couple is emancipated from the mirror frame. The clerk liberates them from

The "extreme" long shot of the interior of Tiffany's.

their financial confinement as well. The couple can only afford to spend ten dollars, but this kind clerk makes a fabulous suggestion. He says that Tiffany's is happy to engrave a Cracker Jack ring that Paul happens to have in his pocket. Impulsively, Holly kisses him on the cheek.

The following scene at the New York Public Library is symbolic as well. At first, Holly is excited to know that Paul's book, *Nine Lives,* is owned by the library. But she is disappointed when a librarian insists that she be quiet. In contrast to the wide framing that is used to display the openness of Tiffany's, the framing of this scene at the library emphasizes the claustrophobic space. There is no extreme long shot used. Holly's orange coat also looks very out of place in these scenes. As if to emphasize the restrictive nature of the space, Holly says she thinks that Paul's book is a prisoner of the library. The librarian does not allow Paul to sign the book that he authored, and the couple quickly leaves, almost as if they are escaping.

Next, the couple approaches a five-and-ten store with a very colorful display window. It is close to Halloween, and the display includes pictures of black cats. Inspired, Holly and Paul start their trick-or-treating—a playful bit of shoplifting. First, Holly thinks of putting a bowl of goldfish in her fur hat because the orange color of the fish matches her coat. Too difficult. After looking at various things, Holly chooses a cat mask and Paul, of course, a dog mask. Sneaking out (like a cat and a naughty dog), they rush away from the store—from a confined space to the outer world. A policeman is standing at the corner, but they surprise him with their masks and run away. The great escape of the cat and the dog is a success. Even when they come back

The cat and the dog.

to their building, they are not captured and framed in the space between two doors at the entrance. There is no high-angle shot from the ceiling that emphasizes the sense of confinement here. For the first time, Holly carries the key. The two take off their masks and kiss for the first time. In a close-up, there is nothing to separate them.

## Return of the Framed World

But escape is not so easy. As the story continues, once again framing and coloring emphasize the captured condition of Holly in particular. The following morning, Paul has an experience that makes him doubt the sense of liberation that he had the day before. After waking up, Paul puts on the dog mask again and visits Holly's room from the emergency window. But her cat does not welcome him; instead, Cat threatens him. The cat usually gets on his shoulders, but today Paul is treated like an uninvited guest.

Paul sees 2E approaching the building, and he rushes back to his apartment. He acts like a scared dog that does not want to be scolded by its master for going out without permission. 2E comes into his apartment, finds Holly's cat mask, scornfully puts it on her face, and then throws it away. The mask is a precious symbol of escape for Holly, though. Infuriated, Paul bids farewell to 2E. He leaves the apartment, saying that he will never again put on the suits (or straitjackets?) that she has given him.

Paul appears to succeed in his escape, even though it means he becomes homeless. But what about Holly? Paul sees someone who looks like her in front of the New York Public Library. He can scarcely believe it, but he follows her back into the library from which he escaped with her the day before. He finds her in the reading room where his book is kept. Bookshelves and monotonous objects within the claustrophobic framing surround her in a long shot. But why is she there? Holly said she did not like the place at all the day before. She wore a vivid orange coat then, but now she has on a very plain beige dress. Even though she is inside a building, she wears black sunglasses while reading a book. Paul cannot understand what is going on. Doesn't she want to escape with him? Paul desperately tells her that he loves her, but Holly resists and says, "Let me go!"

Holly appears to be conflicted, caught between the framed world and the prospect of liberation from it. She is confused by the appearance of a person who seems to love her not as a pet but as a person for the first time. She may have stepped out of her "free" and egocentric life and started reading his book at the library in order to understand Paul as a person. But it is not easy to truly escape from the framed world. Indeed, cats love small and confined spaces even though they seem to move around freely all the time. They were originally wild animals living in mountains and woods that were full of dangers, so they may feel safe when they can hide themselves in small spaces—or, in this case, the framed world. As I mentioned earlier, Holly's cat likes the small sink in the kitchen best.

Holly goes back to the life that she is used to and starts chasing "rats" again. José, a rich Brazilian, is her next target. When Paul visits Holly's place several days later, she is knitting and practicing Portuguese with a record player. Holly says she has decided to go to Brazil with José, but Paul gradually finds out that she is not marrying him but only being "kept" by him as a lover. At this very moment, a pressure cooker explodes in the kitchen. It is as if the food inside has tried to escape its confinement. Does this indicate that Holly's true wish is to escape from her life of being kept as a pet even though she appears to be jumping into a new "pet" situation with José?

Holly and Paul decide to eat out and walk the city together once again. A low-angle shot of the couple emphasizes how the lattice made by numerous windows surrounds them from all directions, like a cage. During the escape scene after they visited Tiffany's and the five-and-ten, the sky was wide open. In contrast, the claustrophobic framing of this exterior scene is the opposite. Holly now says, "Oh, I love New York." But she does not sound happy. It sounds as if she is trying to convince herself.

When they return to the apartment building, they are handcuffed by the police and literally become prisoners. Holly carries six keys so as not to be caught between the two doors of the entrance, but they are useless with the handcuffs. The police and Yuniyoshi have been waiting for them because they are suspected of cooperating in the crimes of the Italian mafia.

"I love New York!"

## Happy Ending = Happy Beginning

Can Holly and Paul escape from their prisons, or the framed world, in the end? Paul comes to pick up Holly by taxi when her charge is dropped. He has brought many of her belongings, including her cat, with him because he thinks it is a good idea for Holly to stay away from her apartment for a while. In the shots on the back seat of the taxi, the couple is framed tightly in a very confined space. Paul tells her that she should give up going to Brazil. Holly's monotone colors emphasize her resistance—a black dress, black stockings, and an off-white trench coat. She tries unsuccessfully to use a red lipstick; her hand shakes, and she is unable to add color to her lips.

Holly screams, "I don't know who I am. I am like Cat here, a no-name slob." She forces the cat out of the claustrophobically framed space in the taxi. However, the cat, now liberated from Holly, clings to the black metal fence by the sidewalk. The cat appears to be caught in a cage. Or, perhaps it has decided to be captured in the framed world. The cat does not leave even when it becomes drenched in heavy rain.

Paul responds, "You call yourself a free spirit, a wild thing. You're terrified somebody's going to stick you in a cage. Well, baby, you're already in that cage. You built it yourself." It may, indeed, be safer for Holly to stay in her cage; it is tough to break away from the framed world. And of course Paul, too, has been in a cage that he built himself. Paul tosses a box to Holly and gets out of the taxi. Inside the box is the Cracker Jack ring they had engraved at Tiffany's with their ten dollars.

Holly starts crying when she looks at the ring. Tears that she has tried not to show pour out of her eyes. Of course, she has known that she has not been free and wild; she understands that she has been in a cage. But she has finally met a person who points that out to her. For the first time, she believes that she and Paul can go out to the world outside together and go after "the same rainbow's end," referred to in the lyrics of "Moon River," the film's theme song.

Putting on the ring, Holly jumps out of the taxi, out of the claustrophobic framing. To the strains of "Moon River," which plays in a minor key, she runs into the pouring rain. Drenched, Holly appears to be crying with her whole body; the rain is her tears. She runs to the alley where she has left her cat and calls to it over and over again, but the cat is nowhere to be found. When she has almost given up, she hears the cat's meow. The cat is shown in a close-up as "Moon River" goes back to a major key. Paul reappears now and embraces Holly and the cat. They kiss in the pouring rain.

We the viewers know that the world outside will surely try to frame these two. As the camera retreats, we see the sky behind them. In this extreme

Happy ending = Happy beginning.

long shot, the sky is not bright; it does not seem to be foretelling a bright future. In contrast to the image of Fifth Avenue in the beautifully vague morning light in the opening scene, what we see now is a dark alley filled with garbage bins and surrounded by dirty buildings. In the framing of this extreme long shot, the couple and the cat still look very confined in the valley of buildings. We know that there will be no more lavish parties. No more Givenchy dresses. Tiffany's jewelry is out of the question. The Cracker Jack ring may be the only jewelry that they can afford unless Paul becomes a bestselling novelist.

Even so, their bodies are sparkling in the pouring rain. A bright female chorus is heard with the score of "Moon River," which seems to indicate hope for the couple's future even though their lives might be tough. Holly, a call girl who has been wandering the city of New York like a stray cat, will become a human being. Together with Paul, she will live independently, not as someone's pet, even if it is in a dirty alley. Probably the cat will finally have its own name; it, too, will go from nobody to somebody. Then, Holly will never say, "I am like cat here, a no-name slob," again. Her life and the cat's life will become independent. The future is not fully bright, but this is still a happy ending, or rather, a happy beginning.

## Framing Hollywood Cinema in Sexual Morality

There is no ending like this in Capote's novel. In the novel, Holly leaves New York for Brazil. She is said to have been seen somewhere in Africa, where she must be still chasing "rats." In contrast, in the film version, Holly will most likely marry Paul and build a family because she has put on the ring. Leaving the wildcat-like "polygamous" situation behind, she will start a new life as a monogamous human being.

Because of this moralistic ending, in which the two protagonists find their true love and seem poised to start a family, *Breakfast at Tiffany's* was able to be produced despite its main characters including prostitutes and mistresses and despite its critical view toward the American society of the period, which confined people with financial hardships. It is also possible that this ending had to be added to ensure its successful production.

Still, it was unusual in the earlier days of Hollywood cinema for a prostitute to have a happy ending even if she made a moralistic choice. A year before the premiere of *Breakfast at Tiffany's* at Radio City Music Hall, *The World of Susie Wong* (Richard Kwan, 1959) was released at the same venue. Its protagonist, also a prostitute, needed to be portrayed as having a "heart of gold." Had the filmmakers not emphasized the moral aspect of the character, it is unlikely that the film would have been released. Interestingly, *The Children's Hour* (William Wyler, 1961), Hepburn's next film, dealt with the issue of lesbianism. As such, by the early 1960s, Hollywood's self-regulation in matters of sex had gradually softened.

It is said that Capote wanted the voluptuous Marilyn Monroe to play Holly instead of the slender Audrey Hepburn. I have no doubt that if the glamorous Monroe had played Holly, she, too, could have conveyed a sense of being captured like a cat in a big city. In fact, in the film, *Don't Bother to Knock* (Roy Ward Baker, 1952), Monroe delicately plays a young woman with a mental problem who has just arrived in New York from the countryside. A pilot played by Richard Widmark first looks at her in a room across a stairwell in a skyscraper hotel, and, like Holly, she is seen framed in a square window.

Hepburn was a perfect fit for the catlike Holly in this film, but Monroe might have been similarly fascinating. If the latter had played the part, however, I think she would have looked more like a fluffy Maine Coon.

# CHAPTER 2

# Cats Love Dark Places

## Lighting in *Cat People*

*Jacques Tourneur, USA, 1942*

### *Breakfast at Tiffany's* and *Cat People*

If *Breakfast at Tiffany's* is the story of a cat-like young woman, then *Cat People* is about a young woman (Simone Simon) who is, in fact, a cat. The story of *Breakfast at Tiffany's* closes with the happy ending of a young couple's marriage. *Cat People* begins with a marriage that is not really happy. While *Breakfast at Tiffany's* depicts the beginning of a couple's journey from a confined monochrome world to a liberated colorful world, *Cat People* shows the tragic failure of such a journey. One is a romantic comedy and the other is a horror movie; the former was produced twenty years after the latter.

Still, these two films are like sisters. Both are set in New York City. The heroines are non native New Yorkers and outsiders (Holly is from Texas; Irena is from Serbia). They are both haunted by the past (Holly was married to an elderly veterinarian in Texas; Irena believes that she is a descendent of the cat people of Serbia). In both films, young men fall in love with the heroines at first sight and try to save them. But both young men are engaged to other women, which makes for triangular relationships. While *Breakfast at Tiffany's* uses framing to emphasize Holly's confinement in small spaces, *Cat People* uses lighting to show the heroine's entrapment in dark places. *Breakfast at Tiffany's* makes us realize that the world of cinema begins in the square frame of the screen. *Cat People* makes us remember that cinema is made of light and shadow.

Cinema is a medium of light. It does not exist without the electrical light beam that passes through the celluloid strip to throw an image onto a screen before a viewer. Even before the process of projection, the production of moving photographic images was a construction in light. Without light, the location, set, costume, and make-up, as well as the actors' expressions and performances, are invisible to the viewer.

At the very beginning of the history of cinema in the late nineteenth century and the early twentieth century, the primary purpose of lighting in cinema was to provide visibility. For instance, "Clarity first, story second" (*ichi nuke, ni suji*), the slogan introduced in the first decade of the twentieth century by Makino Shōzō, "the father of Japanese cinema," clearly indicates the importance of light and lighting in the early period of filmmaking. As the term *nuke* (clarity) suggests, what early Japanese filmmakers emphasized was not the expressivity of artificial lighting but the brightness itself, which would make images visible even in worn-out prints screened at theaters not equipped with bright light bulbs for projection. The priority was to make actors and sets visible to the audience. Hollywood films were lit in the same manner, making particular use of sunlight, until around 1915.

American filmmakers started to consider this style of lighting to be old-fashioned only a few years later. Most likely inspired by theatrical lighting, filmmakers became aware of the expressive effects of strong, weak, frontal, back, top, bottom, and side lighting, and the shadows that lighting creates. The impact of lighting is immense for the narrative, the atmosphere and mood of scenes, and the psychology and emotion of characters, among other elements. Inevitably, the use of light and technologies of lighting started to occupy the center of discussions in filmmaking. In April 1934, Earl Theisen, the honorary curator of The Academy Museum of Motion Pictures, wrote in *International Photographer*, the journal for Hollywood's cinematographers' union, "The most important of the dramatic devices of the motion picture is light. Light and shade are the most vital of the cinematic tools. Emotions are literally painted with light" (Theisen 1934, 10).

*Cat People* appears to be a horror film with monster cats. But producer Val Lewton does not make a film in which a fake monster ostentatiously appears; instead, he tells a tragic love story. The title sounds like a remake of *The Wolf Man* (George Wagner, 1941), in which a hero turns into a werewolf after he is attacked and bitten by a wolf-like creature of folklore. But in contrast to *The Wolf Man,* it is not really important in *Cat People* to show how the heroine turns into a cat person or to explain what kind of monsters the cat people are. Instead, the film focuses on the sorrow of a young cat person who happens to fall in love with a human.

Director Jacques Tourneur and cinematographer Nicholas Musuraca, in particular, responded with conspicuous use of lighting in this film. Early film theorist Rudolph Arnheim claimed, "[T]he use of shading does not necessarily originate from the observation of nature, and certainly is not always used in accordance with the rules of illumination" (Arnheim 1974, 321). Tourneur and Musuraca emphasized that artificial lighting is essential to cinema. Constructing shadows with lighting, *Cat People* sensitively expresses the heroine's pain that the man she loves cannot understand what she really is.

Without any special publicity, the film became a word-of-mouth hit after it was released on Friday the thirteenth in November 1942 and stayed at theaters in Hollywood for thirteen weeks (Newman 1999, 64). Even *Citizen Kane* (Orson Welles, 1941), which was released in the previous year to great fanfare, played for only twelve weeks. Clearly many people were caught up in the fate of Irena, eloquently expressed in the play of light and shadow.

## Irena Loves Dark Places: Three-point Lighting and Lasky Lighting

*Cat People* begins with a picture of a black panther. After the credits of cast, staff, and director, a cheerful accordion tune takes the place of the orchestral theme score. The tune is played at the Central Park Zoo, where the story begins. A black panther paces in a cage. As the camera retreats, we see Irena, the heroine of this film, eagerly making sketches in front of the cage. Her mouth is pointed and her eyes are a little separated from each other. Her face looks like a kitten's. Simone Simon, who plays Irena, was a French actress who had appeared in Jean Renoir's *La Bête humaine* (1938) two years before in the role of a young wife with a kitten.

Irena (Simone Simon) sketches a black panther at the Central Park Zoo.

Irena tears up a sketch she does not like and throws it toward a hollow tree stump that serves as a waste-bin. Oliver (Kent Smith), a young marine engineer, sees the paper miss the bin and warns Irena about it. It seems that both are favorably disposed to each other. But Irena does not seem to care for Oliver's moralistic advice: "Let no one say, and say to your shame, that all was beauty here before you came." Does he mean that the public morality of a human society doesn't affect cats? This scene of the first encounter between Irena and Oliver ends with a close-up of another sketch thrown away by Irena. It drops on to the street, is blown away by a gust, and stops at a fence. The sketch shows a black panther stabbed by a stiletto. The panther's cage, which is not seen on the screen, creates a dark shadow on the paper. The lighting, together with the score, which suddenly changes to a minor key, adds an ominous tone to the future of the couple that has just met. As such, from the very beginning, artificial lighting and constructed shadows play a significant role to develop the narrative and formulate certain moods for the scenes in *Cat People*.

We should note one more significant thing in this opening scene: it shows that Oliver is the kind of man who starts flirting with another woman without a word to the woman he is with. There is a woman right next to Oliver, drinking Coca-Cola with him. We only see her back, but her suit, blonde hair, and hairstyle indicate that this is Alice ( Jane Randolph), who appears again later in the film. Alice is Oliver's colleague at the marine engineering office, and she is secretly in love with him. While a love triangle will be formed along the way,

A dark shadow appears on Irena's sketch of a black panther.

there is no shadow cast on Alice, a very cheerful woman, at this opening scene. She simply stands under the sun in this exterior scene, in flat lighting (even lighting on a subject, producing little contrast or shadow).

The shadows become thicker after Irena and Oliver enter the apartment building where Irena lives. In a long shot of the two standing at the entrance, the handrail of a long staircase and the window frames create strong lattice-shaped shadows on their faces and bodies because of the sunlight coming in from the windows. Irena has been joyfully conversing with Oliver up to this point but shows her first hesitation in those shadows. "I've never had anyone here. You're the first friend I meet [sic] in America. Oh, I know lots of people in business. Editors, secretaries, other sketch artists, you know. But you might be my first real friend." Irena's words signal her shyness and anxiety at being alone with a man in a foreign land. Oliver, though, is enraptured by the fact that he has been invited into an apartment by a woman whom he has just met. He merely smiles at Irena.

The first close-up of Irena in this film follows. This may be regarded as an image of how Irena appears in Oliver's eyes. This is because all the shadows on her face in the previous long shot are completely gone. Three-point lighting, which Hollywood cinema perfected in the 1920s in order to show off the beauty and glamour of their stars, makes Irena's hair, eyes, and face glow softly but gorgeously. Three-point lighting consists of three lights—key light, fill light, and backlight. The key light brings the primary light to the subject and highlights the form and dimension of it. It is not

Long shot of Irena and Oliver in the shadowy apartment building.

placed directly in front of the subject but instead slightly off to the side. The hard (or focused) key light clearly illuminates the contours of the subject, in this case, Irena's face, and creates the splendor of her eyes. But as it is, the rectangular angle of the light beam in relation to the subject also creates darkly shaded areas on the subject, in this case on Irena's face, because of her nose, cheekbones, etc. The fill light, usually a soft and indirect supplementary light that does not change the character of the key light, is used to erase darkly shaded areas on the subject, in this case again Irena's face. The fill light is usually placed at a vertical angle to the key light. The fill light allows room for controlling the appearance of the subject. The dimmer the fill light is, the harsher the subject looks. In this case, Irena's face does not look harsh at all, compared to the more contrasty long shot that precedes. Finally, the backlight, which is placed behind the subject at a slightly higher angle in order not to be seen by the camera, distinguishes the subject from her background and provides a sense of three-dimensionality. In this case, Irena's face is clearly distinguished from the darker background. In addition, and more importantly, the backlight gives a halo effect to her hair. Along with the glamorous effect that the three-point lighting brings to this close-up of Irena's face, a romantic tune is heard.

*Casablanca* (Michael Curtiz, 1942), which was released in the same year as *Cat People,* is another film that utilizes three-point lighting effectively in order to depict the glamour of the heroine. Ilsa (Ingrid Bergman) tells Sam the pianist (Dooley Wilson), "Play it, Sam," and implores him to play

Close-up of Irena in three-point lighting.

"As Time Goes By." Hearing the tune that he has forbidden Sam to play, Rick storms over in fury. There he sees Ilsa in a close-up. A spotlight illuminates her eyes, which are blurred by tears, and her lips, which are slightly open; a fill light softly embraces her face, and a backlight gives an almost sacred glow to the blonde hair of Bergman, who was originally from Northern Europe. In the background, we hear more romanticized orchestral sound swelling over the sound of Sam's piano, hinting that Rick is idealizing Ilsa here.

In *Cat People,* Irena does not stay in the soft three-point light for long. As soon as she opens the door of her apartment and the two enter, we move to the next scene. Irena's room is in darkness. Weak light from streetlamps and a building across the street enters the room through windows at the back. A statue of a man on horseback on a table is in silhouette. The man holds a raised sword, upon which a cat is speared. Standing by the table, Irena hums a gentle tune and explains. The man on the horse is King John of Serbia. The cat pierced by his sword is a symbol of the Mumluks, who worshiped Satan and made the people slaves. When King John drove out the Mumluks, some escaped into dark mountain villages. Irena says she is a descendent of one of those villages, which has become steeped in the legends of witchcraft. She murmurs, "I like the dark. It's friendly." Contrary to the ideal image created by the three-point lighting, presumably from Oliver's point of view, Irena appears to be herself in shadows.

Indeed, cats love dark places. Cats are nocturnal. They are more active during nighttime hours than during the day. Cats are originally from mountains and forests, where the sunlight is dim. Anyone who has lived with a cat has experienced finding his or her cat sleeping in a closet or a drawer. Surprising but funny. They feel very comfortable in those dark places, and the black pupils of their eyes become wide open and round. They look cute, but if we see them on a dark street, their gleaming eyes can be scary, too.

Unlike the glamorous splendor of the three-point lighting in the previous scene, Irena is here lit by so-called Lasky lighting, in which not only light but also shadow are conspicuous. As in a Rembrandt painting, a spotlight is directed to a limited area within a frame, which not only creates clear shadows but also indicates the source and direction of light. Around 1915, when cinema was silent, Cecil B. DeMille, who would later direct such spectacular films as *The Ten Commandments* (1956), and his cinematographer Alvin Wyckoff developed a lighting style with strong contrasts in order to create dramatic effects in cinema. Adopting carbon-arc equipment, such as Kliegl spotlights (called klieg lights), in particular, DeMille and Wyckoff moved the film lighting practice in Hollywood away from a dominant use of diffused, overall illumination toward a concentration on "effects" lighting (Bordwell,

Sessue Hayakawa in Lasky Lighting.

Steiger, and Thompson 1985, 223). In particular, they used "spotlights . . . to produce low-key lighting effects in several productions" (Bordwell, Steiger, and Thompson 1985, 224–225). Their lighting style was called Lasky lighting, which film historian Lea Jacobs defines as "confined and shallow areas of illumination, sharp-edged shadows and a palpable sense of the directionality of light" (Jacobs 1993, 408).

DeMille and Wyckoff had contracts with the Jesse L. Lasky Feature Play Company at that time. DeMille had a background in theater and brought the lighting techniques of the theatrical stage to cinema. Lasky lighting was directly derived from a popular theater lighting style developed by David Belasco, who was inspired by Rembrandt's treatment of light that emphasized the source of light from windows, lamps, or fires and created a dark atmosphere. Sessue Hayakawa became the biggest Asian star in the history of Hollywood cinema in part because of Lasky lighting. In *The Cheat* (1915), a masterpiece by DeMille and Wyckoff, dramatic lighting with strong contrasts enhanced the exotic and mysterious atmosphere surrounding Hayakawa's villain, giving a pleasurable shock to many female spectators.

Despite the impact of Lasky lighting, it did not become the mainstream lighting of Hollywood cinema because the contrasts of light and shadow it created were too extreme. By the 1920s, the majority of Hollywood lighting had become bright and soft, without conspicuous contrast between lights and shadow. Three-point lighting emerged as part of that trend. While major characters and props that viewers should not overlook are clearly visible, such lighting is not so obvious that viewers are even aware of it, which focuses attention on the story of the film. Lasky lighting that emphasized shadows fell into a secondary position, used to add effects to gangster genres, among others, that Warner Bros. was particularly good at.

In the 1940s, when *Cat People* was produced, Lasky lighting was revived in the films that would later be called "film noir," which I will discuss in more detail in chapter five. In film noir, the lighting was favorably used to dramatically and realistically express the obsession or insanity of protagonists who often became involved with urban crimes. RKO Radio, which produced *Cat People,* also produced a number of films noirs.

In *Cat People,* Lasky lighting is effectively used in Irena's room. Behind Irena, Goya's 1784 painting, *Boy with Cats* (*Manuel Osorio Manrique de Zúñiga*), hangs on the wall; in it, three cats gaze at a little bird from the dark. Their eyes glow ominously, lit by a spotlight. In the following close-up of Irena's face, her left eye is strongly lit and shines ominously. The shining eyes of the cats and Irena form some kind of a connection in the dark. Such lighting makes us, the viewers, wonder whether the story about witches and cat people is only Irena's wild fantasy, or not.

After this scene, the love affair between the heroine and the hero literally turns into a battle between light and shadow. It is also one of three-point

Irena in front of a Goya painting.

Irena's left eye is strongly lit and shines ominously.

lighting versus Lasky lighting under the strict scheme of cinematographer Nicholas Musuraca, who would work on a number of masterpieces of film noir after this film, including *Out of the Past* (1947), directed by Jacques Tourneur. Can Oliver become Irena's "first real friend"? Can he live with her in the dark that she likes? Or, is he going to make her into the ideal shining image that he has of her? And will he forcefully try to bring her into the bright world that he likes?

Then the clock shows six o'clock. Oliver realizes that he has stayed too long. He promises to have dinner with Irena the following day and leaves her room. A truce. The battle of love and the battle of light and shadow have just begun.

## Oliver Likes Bright Places

Unlike Irena's dark apartment, Oliver's marine engineering office is very bright. Except for the soft shadows of the circular frames of the chic, high windows, created by the sunlight on the wall, the spacious room is lit brightly and flatly. This is a typical lighting scheme of 1930s Hollywood cinema. A number of people are working cheerfully in the room. Alice is one of them. She notices a kitten's meow. (In fact, the kitten's voice is played by actress Dorothy Lloyd. She is a cat person.) Alice finds a shoebox on Oliver's drawing board and a white kitten inside it. He intends it as a gift for Irena—a bit insensitive, perhaps, for a woman suffering from a "cat curse."

Oliver's bright office.

We quickly learn that there is another cat in Oliver's office. Its name is John Paul Jones, after the American Revolutionary War hero. It is a perfect name for the office cat of a marine engineering firm. At the same time, the name symbolically expresses an American attitude toward foreigners, represented by Oliver. This film never refers explicitly to contemporary political issues. But the time was 1942, in the middle of World War II. The House Un-American Activities Committee (HUAC), which was originally created in 1938, was investigating alleged disloyalty and subversive activities. Anti-foreigner sentiments were stirring. At the same time, a pedagogical policy, or a desire of conquest, to Americanize immigrants from foreign countries, existed. Consciously or not, Oliver, as a typical white American man, seems to have this type of attitude toward Irena. It is true that this film depicts Oliver in a slightly critical manner. This might be because Val Lewton, the producer of this film, was an immigrant from Russia and had experienced discrimination as a foreigner in American society.

Irena has been living in the dark and is anxious about entering the bright world where Oliver lives. But Oliver does not listen to her. "You're here in America. You're so normal, you're in love with me, Oliver Reed, a good plain Americano. You're so normal, you're gonna marry me and those fairy tales, you can tell them to our children. They'll love them." In order not to offend Oliver the American, does Irena the foreigner have to do what he says? America is bright and Serbia is dark, and never the twain shall meet?

"Moia sestra, moia sestra."

## Will Oliver Learn to Like Dark Places?

In the following scene, Irena and Oliver are already married. They are in the midst of their wedding reception at Belgrade, the only Serbian restaurant in New York. Lots of candles stand on the table, which is brightly lit. Irena sits next to Oliver and smiles as "normal" newlywed brides do. It is as if bright America has enlightened dark Serbia.

But suddenly, the dark side strikes back. A woman from another table comes by and speaks to Irena in a foreign language. "Moia sestra, moia sestra," she says. She wears a black dress that shines like a black cat's fur and has a black ribbon in her hair, which looks like cat ears. Irena cannot say a word. With a vague smile, the woman puts a black, hairy scarf over her shoulders and slips out into the snowy, dark street outside. Oliver's colleague whispers, "Looks like a cat." At this moment, Irena clearly remembers that she is not living in the same world as Oliver. With a frozen expression, she says to Oliver, "She called me sister." Because of the appearance of the cat person, their wedding turns out not to be "normal."

Even though it is their wedding night, Irena and Oliver do not sleep together. They do not even kiss each other. In their darkened apartment, a tightly closed door separates them. In Lasky lighting, Irena leans against that door and sits down. She puts her right-hand fingernails onto the door, as cats often do with their claws. A cat's meow is heard from somewhere, too.

Irena sits in a shadow.

"But I want to be Mrs. Reed, really," she says. "I want to be everything that name means to me. And I can't. I can't. Oliver, be kind, be patient. Let me have time. Time to get over that feeling there's something evil in me."

On the other side of the door, in brighter light, Oliver replies, "Darling, you can have all the time there is in the world if you want it and all the patience and kindness there is in me."

But, after all, Oliver cannot be patient enough to wait for this creature from the dark.

Even though she asks Oliver to wait, Irena becomes more and more feline-like after the wedding night. Has her true nature been revealed despite her wish? Or, is she hoping that Oliver will accept her as she is? In any case, the costume, the props, and above all the lighting emphasize her approach to the dark side. Irena starts to wear a short-haired black fur coat, similar to the one the cat person at the restaurant wore. When she visits a museum with Oliver and Alice, she goes close to a statue of Bastet, a cat goddess of ancient Egypt. (In the film, we actually see a statue of Anubis, a jackal-headed god. The director wanted Bastet, but the prop department could not find one.) When she works as a dress designer, she makes a sketch of the cat woman from the restaurant. One day, during her work, she casually stands up, sticks her left hand into a birdcage hung beside a window, and plays with a canary inside. Irena's face is shown in a close-up, and her right eye shines ominously. Her white teeth are slightly visible, too. Cats become excited when they see insects or birds; their pupils dilate and they show their teeth. What we the

Irena stands near a statue of Anubis.

viewers see next is a shot of the canary lying dead in the cage. Did Irena kill it unexpectedly with her hand, just as cats kill other creatures without knowing it when they play with them?

Seeing Irena acting strange, Oliver recommends that she see a psychiatrist called Dr. Judd. He wants Irena to be able to lead a "normal" life in American society. Dr. Judd uses bright lights for the treatment. When he asks questions of Irena, he places a strong, tight spotlight on her face while she lies in the dark.

"You were saying, the cats . . ." he begins, prompting her.

Irena answers with her eyes closed. "They torment me. I wake in the night and the tread of their feet whispers in my brain. I have no peace for they are in me. In me. In me."

After hearing this, Dr. Judd opens the curtain and stands beside Irena in the bright light from outside. "And the cat women of your village, too. You told me of them. Women who, in jealousy or anger or out of their own corrupt passions, can change into great cats, like panthers. And if one of these women were to fall in love and if her lover were to kiss her, take her into his embrace, she would be driven by her own evil to kill him. That's what you believe and fear, isn't it?"

Irena nods.

Window frames create a cross-shaped shadow on the wall. Dr. Judd, taking notes in front of it, looks like a priest with the Bible in his hand. Irena, sitting on a sofa beside him, looks like a believer who needs his guidance.

Irena's face is placed under a strong and tight spotlight.

Jealousy, anger, and passion. These emotions wait for Irena when she comes back from the doctor's office. She opens the door of her apartment and finds the room brighter than usual. She sees Alice lighting her cigarette at the back of the room. While she was away, brightness has been brought into her room by another woman and replaced the darkness that she loves. Irena also finds out that Dr. Judd, who conducts the light treatment, was actually recommended by Alice. At this moment, Irena realizes she is facing an enemy. She wants to face the darkness in her only with Oliver. But light has invaded in the shape of another woman.

## Alice Does Not Like Dark Places

For Irena, Alice becomes an enemy. But to us, the viewers, this is not really true. Rather, Oliver is the one who is to blame. He told Irena that she could have all the time in the world, but after only a short while, he says to Alice, "I've never been unhappy before," and "I don't even know whether I'm in love with Irena." Alice replies right away, "I can't bear to see you unhappy. I love you too darn much, and I don't care if you do know it, Ollie." Here a close-up with the three-point lighting appears again. As in the first close-up of Irena, Alice's blonde hair and tearful eyes shine beautifully. Shown in such an enchanting manner, Alice captures Oliver's heart as well as ours. Alice is not a bitch who steals Oliver from Irena, however. She is always cheerful and loves Oliver earnestly. She is the other heroine of this film. So we sympathize with her.

Alice stands beside an illuminated table.

Irena stops seeing Dr. Judd. It is natural for her to do so because Dr. Judd was recommended by her rival in love. But Oliver loses his temper when he finds out. He says he has some work to do and leaves their apartment. Irena makes up with him and calls his office. It is Alice who picks up the phone. Alice's worktable has a light bulb inside that illuminates her face brightly. In contrast, Irena hangs up in darkness without a word. She puts on her black fur coat and leaves the apartment with a hard expression. Alice also leaves the office. When she turns off the table light, she places herself in the dark for the first time in this film.

Alice finds Oliver at a café nearby and joins him. It is the worst possible timing. Irena passes by on her way to their office, looks through the window, and sees Oliver and Alice sitting together. Half of her face is hidden behind the curtain and window frame. Her left eye is ominously lit by the light from the café. The Lasky lighting emphasizes the fire of jealousy.

The shot that follows clearly shows Irena's reflection on the window, which makes it look as though Irena is split into two figures. Does the cat woman reveal itself from inside Irena's body? As closing time approaches, a waitress starts turning off lamps in the café. The office and then the café—both places that are usually bright—gradually go dark. Irena makes sure that the couple leaves the café and goes out onto the dark sidewalk.

As if protecting themselves from the dark, Oliver and Alice stop at the bright spot right under a street lamp.

"You cold?" he asks her.

Irena spots Oliver and Alice, and her eye is fired by jealousy.

Irena is split into two figures.

"A cat just walked over my grave."

Waving goodbye to Oliver, Alice walks into the shadow of Central Park. Now the climactic chase begins. The lighting persistently emphasizes the contrast between light and shadow. The editing creates an intense tempo between the woman who chases and the woman who is being chased. (We will focus on editing in chapter three.) Moreover, the sound heightens tension and adds shock effects. These techniques make this chase scene truly tense, like watching a cat on a hot tin roof.

The camera first captures Alice in a white coat in a long shot. She walks on the pavement, first passing through a lit area under a street lamp, then a dark area in shadow. The hard sound of her high heels on asphalt echoes. Then, the camera switches to Irena in her black fur coat as she follows Alice in a long shot. Exactly like Alice, she walks on the pavement, passing through a lit area under a street lamp and a dark area in shadow to the sound of her high heels. The shot that follows shows Alice's feet in a close-up. Her feet move continuously from light to shadow. We hear her high heels tapping on the pavement.

A close-up of Irena's feet follows. From light to shadow. The sound of high heels. Remembering the silent phone call to the office, Alice starts to feel frightened. She quickens her pace. Tap-tap-tap. Alice does not know who is following her. She does not even realize that Irena thinks of her as her enemy. But it is scary to be followed in the dark. Suddenly, the footsteps that have followed her stop. Noticing that, Alice stops under a street lamp and turns around. She walks again for a few feet and turns around again. All she can see is the deserted pavement, a street lamp, and the darkness. There is no sound at all. Panicked, she is about to start running.

All of a sudden, a hissing sound cuts through the air. At the same time, from the opposite direction, a bus rushes into the frame and makes a sudden stop. Together with Alice, our hearts seem to stop beating. The driver speaks to Alice in a cheerful voice from the bright inside.

"You look as if you'd seen a ghost."

But Alice does not have her usual gay attitude. She responds seriously, "Did you see it?" Then she climbs quickly into the brightly lit bus.

Alice walks.

Irena follows.

Alice gazes at the deserted pavement and the darkness.

After the bus leaves, a black bush sways above the stone wall beside the pavement. The Central Park Zoo is beyond the wall. There is a sheep cage there, in which an alarming event seems to be occurring. A caretaker comes out with a lantern. A sheep has been attacked. The camera goes back to the pavement under a street lamp, where we see the black footprints of a big cat. After a while, the prints change into those of high heels. At the same time, we start to hear the sound of footsteps again. Tap-tap-tap. Then,

Irena cries in a bathtub.

Irena appears out of the darkness. She is placing a white handkerchief on her mouth. Is she wiping away blood from a sheep that she has just attacked? All of a sudden, a taxi makes a quick stop nearby with a hissing sound, which makes us jump once again.

Coming back to the apartment, Irena finds Oliver there but ignores him. She takes off her stockings, fills the bathtub, and climbs in. Under the bright light of the bathroom, drops of water shine on her naked back. She holds her knees tightly and cries. It is a shocking revelation. She *is* a cat person. This is the first time that Irena voluntarily places herself under bright light, but she looks more distraught than ever. It seems as if she wants to be cleansed by the light. This is the most excruciating shot in this film.

In 1942, when *Cat People* was released, the content that could be shown in films was controlled by the Production Code. As discussed in the previous chapter, showing nudity on the screen was severely controlled. Film critic Kim Newman claims, "This affecting little vignette must have been fairly risqué for 1942: Simone Simon stripping her stockings and exposing a little naked back in a non-sexual situation wouldn't have counted as 'hot stuff' before the imposition of the Production Code in 1934, but here it indicates Lewton's intention to push the envelope on censorship" (Newman 1999, 46). Looking at Irena's naked back, people watching this film in 1942 must have felt that they had just seen what they should not. That makes this scene even more painful.

When the dark night falls, Irena cannot help chasing Alice again; it is, after all, a cat's nature to pursue its prey. Alice is going to exercise at a YWCA swimming pool. A black cat follows her from the front desk when she goes downstairs to the locker room. Following the black cat, Irena in her black fur coat appears at the front desk without a sound and asks the woman there where she can find Alice. In the locker room, Alice, now in a bathing suit, happens to look up the stairway. She sees a moving shadow of a panther-like creature. The shadow is too big for the black cat at the front desk. Panicked, Alice jumps head first into the brightly lit pool. At that moment, the growl of a panther begins.

Floating in the middle of the pool, Alice looks around the poolside. The light leaking from the locker room is reflected on the water and creates various shadows on the walls and the ceiling. Those shadows ominously keep moving. The whole room becomes dark for a moment. Something has blocked the light from the locker room. It becomes light, and then dark again. Alice is desperately treading water and cannot clearly see what it is. All she can see is the light and the shadow swaying on the wall and the ceiling. A shot of Alice in the pool and a shot of the light and the shadow on the wall and the ceiling are repeated. The shot lengths become shorter and shorter. Then, a clear shadow of a panther moves at the poolside. (During the actual shooting, a panther was never used. Director Jacques Tourneur created the shadow with his fists.) Alice screams. A shot of the poolside. A shot of the light and the shadow on the ceiling. Alice desperately moves her arms and legs in panic. Because of Alice's frantic movements, the swaying light and shadow on the wall and the ceiling move much more quickly and haphazardly. All of a sudden, Irena appears at the poolside. She turns on the light and looks down at Alice.

"What is the matter, Alice?"

Alice screams in the swimming pool.

The light and the shadow swaying on the wall.

Cats hate water. Of course, there are some cats, including mine, that play with water dripping from faucets or scoop water from a bowl to drink. But I do not think there are many cats that like to bathe in a bathtub or in a swimming pool. I am sure that I'm not the only person who, trying to wash a cat in a bathtub, has been resisted with unbelievable strength, and has been scratched by their claws. Such experiences are traumatic for both cats and human beings.

Most likely because Alice was in the water, Irena could not catch her game again. Instead, Alice's bathrobe, left in the locker room, becomes the victim. It has been torn to pieces. Now Alice clearly knows. She is Irena's target, and Irena is a brutal cat woman.

## Irena's Death: Can I Leave the Dark Place Now?

"I love Alice. Irena, it's too late . . . Well, there seems only one decent thing for me to do. I'll give you a divorce. Believe me, it's better this way," Oliver tells Irena when she comes home.

"Better? Better for whom?"

Oliver cannot answer. He leaves the dark apartment. Left alone, Irena crawls on hands and knees and buries her face in a sofa. Fire rises up in the fireplace. The contrast between light and shadow becomes stronger because of the firelight. At that moment, Irena's right fingers rip the sofa.

Oliver finds Alice at the office. Unlike Irena's dark room, the drawing table of his office emits bright light and illuminates them brightly. The phone rings. Shortly after, a shadow of a panther appears on the office wall, and the growl is heard, too. Irena is back again to chase Alice. This time there is no place to escape—no bus and no swimming pool. The only thing in hand that can become a weapon is a t-shaped ruler for drawing. All Oliver and Alice can do is place themselves in the light and pray. As Kim Newman describes, "With the strong underlighting from the drafting tables shining merciless spotlights on Oliver and Alice as they back into a corner, the scene uses light as inventively as shadow to terrify. The cat inhabits pools of dark low-down in the room, prowling between items of furniture, but its potential prey are frozen in harsh, bright whiteness against the walls" (Newman 1999, 59).

Covered by the bright light from the drawing table, Oliver says. "Leave us, Irena. In the name of God, leave us in peace." The t-shaped ruler in his hand creates a cross-like shadow on the wall. The shadow of a panther circles around the couple in the bright light. Is she hesitating? For Irena, Alice is an enemy. But how about Oliver? She has hoped he would accept her as she is, someone who cannot help living in a dark place. She has tried to become fond of bright places so they could live a "normal" life together. After a little while, the shadow of the panther, or the shadow of Irena as a cat person, vanishes from the office as if it has forgiven the couple in the light.

Irena goes back home alone. But Dr. Judd waits for her there. Irena's face in a close-up is lit by the three-point lighting. It is a beautiful image of Irena as seen through Dr. Judd's lustful eyes. But in the extreme close-up of Irena's face that follows, the lighting has clearly changed. It is Lasky lighting

"Leave us, Irena. In the name of God, leave us in peace."

The t-shaped ruler in Oliver's hand creates a cross-like shadow on the wall.

Close-up of Irena in the three-point lighting.

with stronger contrasts. Irena's face is in shadow now. Ominous light dwells in her eyes. She has forgotten Oliver and spared Alice. But now she must face the one who uses light to hypnotize her and invades her territory of darkness. This is the final battle of shadow against light. A black shadow of a panther attacks Dr. Judd, who defends himself with a sword cane.

Fatally injured, Irena heads to the dark and misty Central Park Zoo. She opens the cage to let the black panther escape. Then she falls down.

Close-up of Irena in Lasky lighting.

Irena's body lies under the bright street lamp.

The blade of Dr. Judd's sword cane is in her shoulder and reflects light dully. Oliver and Alice arrive, and the love triangle ends where it all began. Irena's body is lying on the pavement under the bright street lamp. Only when she dies is she able to give herself to bright light.

Oliver murmurs, "She never lied to us." Only when she dies is she understood by Oliver. The panther that has escaped also dies. The moment he jumps out into the city of New York, he is hit by a car. Its dead body is also brightly lit by the car's headlight.

The two inhabitants of the bright world, Oliver and Alice, are united as an American couple. The monster from a foreign country who lives in the dark is gone. But is this a happy ending? In the end, Oliver could not believe. He could not wait. Fully utilizing artificial lighting and constructing shadows, *Cat People* tells a story about light and shadow that cannot live happily ever after.

# CHAPTER 3

# Cats Love Chases

## Editing in *To Catch a Thief*

*Alfred Hitchcock, USA, 1955*

### Cary Grant Is the Cat

If *Breakfast at Tiffany's* and *Cat People* are stories about female cats, *To Catch a Thief*, a romantic comedy that Alfred Hitchcock directed in Southern France, is that of a male cat. Cary Grant plays the role of John Robie, who was once a notorious burglar called "The Cat."

Grant already had a close cinematic connection to cats—he had starred in a hilarious comedy about a pet panther, *Bringing Up Baby* (Howard Hawks) in 1938. Despite his masculine figure and gentle appearance, Grant was once a vaudeville acrobat, and this agility makes him perfect for the role of "The Cat." He carries himself well, moving steadily on tiled roofs. So does Brigitte Auber, who plays Danielle, a young French woman, and who also had experience as an acrobat. The climactic rooftop chase between Grant and Auber is the highlight of *To Catch a Thief.*

As Holly of *Breakfast at Tiffany's* aspires to be liberated, the most precious thing in life for The Cat is to be free. Before World War II, Robie was a jewel thief in Paris. According to his own account, he never worked in a group but always acted alone. He was once caught and imprisoned but escaped when the war began and the prison was destroyed in a Nazi attack. He participated in the Resistance, fighting the Nazi occupation, which of course deprived many millions of people of freedom. But he claims no righteousness for his work as a thief; rather, he calmly relates how he kept all the money he stole for himself in order to eat the delicious food he preferred whenever he wishes. Now he is retired and lives alone, free from worldly cares, at a luxurious mountain villa that overlooks the Côte d'Azur. Cats love high places.

A black cat prowls.

Robie hears news of jewel robberies taking place at luxury hotels and is surprised. Every night, a thief appears on the roof, steals jewelry from dark hotel rooms, and leaves again via the roof. In order to convey the thief's light moves, the camera shows a black cat coming and going on the roof—or is he actually leading the thief? Except for a pair of black gloves stealthily taking the jewels, we the viewers cannot see who this thief is in this opening scene. The only thing left behind is the outcries of the ladies whose jewelry has been stolen.

Robie becomes the suspect right away because the modus operandi of the robberies is very similar to his signature style. We see a black cat sitting on a sofa in Robie's house. Even though this black cat is asleep for now, it looks as though he has been in a bad mood. The headline of a newspaper on the sofa reads "The Cat Prowls Again?" and the paper has been torn by a claw. Is the cat irritated, perhaps, by the appearance of an imposter of his master? In order to catch the new "Cat" and clear his name, Robie begins an investigation of his own.

Superficially, *To Catch a Thief* is about the real Cat coming back to chase the false Cat. Indeed, cats love to chase. My own two cats begin a chase in my apartment out of the blue when they are refueled with food or something stimulates them. They run upstairs at full speed, jump on cat trees, and grapple with each other. They look like they're fighting because they hiss and growl at each other. But the next moment, they will be licking each other affectionately. They apparently love chasing each other.

The interesting thing about this film is that the one who is chasing is also being chased at the same time. Robie is chased by the police as a suspect in the jewel robberies. He is also a target of both Francie (Grace Kelly), the daughter of a deceased Texas oil king, and Danielle, a French girl working

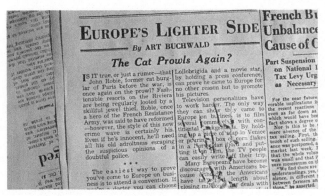

The newspaper is torn by a cat's claws.

at a local restaurant. Both are young, jealous, and primed for romance. They are trying to catch the male cat who loves freedom and make him a lovely pet, or a husband. Among his pursuers we can also count Mrs. Stevens (Jessie Royce Landis), widow of the oil king and Francie's mother, who is happy to buy Robie for her daughter regardless of cost. Thus, *To Catch a Thief* is about chases on multiple levels. Hitchcock himself said in an interview a few years before the release of *To Catch a Thief,* "Well, for one thing, the chase seems to me the final expression of the motion picture medium" (Gottlieb 1995, 125). If so, *To Catch a Thief* is one of Hitchcock's ultimate films.

## Editing of the Chase: Crosscutting

The chase is the basis of cinema. The action film genre, in particular, has existed since the very beginning of the history of cinema. For instance, *The Great Train Robbery* (Edwin S. Porter, 1903), arguably the first narrative film, is about a chase between a steam locomotive seized by a gang of robbers and a group of sheriffs on horseback. Even in the *Star Wars* saga, the epitome of contemporary mega-hits, the most thrilling scene of all is the chase between the Rebel Force, including the Millennium Falcon commanded by Han Solo (Harrison Ford), and the imperial battleships.

Along with the chase came editing, the essential technique in cinema, which developed together with framing and lighting. Editing is a technique that connects two shots that were photographed at different times and places to create some kind of a story. (A shot consists of the film that is exposed from the time the camera is started to the time it is stopped.) It is very difficult to show the chaser and the chased in the square frame of the screen at the same time, especially if they are widely separated. It is possible for the camera to capture the two actors in a single shot if it is placed at a distance or moves from one person to the other. But viewers will not fully experience the actors' speed or tension with either of these techniques, no matter how fast those two people are actually running.

The editing technique called "crosscutting" developed as one method for overcoming this difficulty. Crosscutting helps to establish that seemingly separate actions are occurring at the same time. For instance, the camera captures two running people in two separate shots. If the camera cuts away from one action to the other and shows these two shots by turns, one seems to be chasing the other even though the two are never in the same shot together. The shorter a shot, the more intense the tension becomes.

The scene in Central Park at night in *Cat People,* which I analyzed in the previous chapter, is a typical example of crosscutting. Because Irena and Alice are shown by turns, the tension of the scene is heightened. Brief shots appear one after another and create the sense of speed. Close-ups can also be included in a crosscut to emphasize nervous or frightened expressions.

Editing also involves sound. To return to the example of *Cat People,* we see Alice running away from the sound of high heels following her. When the sound stops, Alice turns back. The following shot shows the deserted pavement, a street lamp, and the darkness beyond in silence. Thus, editing— both visual and audio—craftily manipulates time and space by shortening shots or by zooming in on objects. As a result, this editing technique heightens viewers' tension and emotions.

In the midst of *To Catch a Thief,* there is a car chase between a sports car that the hero and heroine are riding in and the police car that tails them. Crosscutting heightens the tension of the scene. The shots of Robie and Francie's sports car and those of the black police car appear in turn. On the one hand, there is Francie, who drives her car at full speed with a superficially calm facial expression. By her side, Robie cannot help clasping his sweaty hands in a close-up and looking down at the cliff right next to the car. On the other hand are two detectives desperately chasing the sports car. They have to slam on the brakes as an elderly woman crosses the street with her laundry. Then they try—and fail—to avoid a chicken wandering into the street for no reason. When we hear the unmistakable sounds of a car crash, we know that the chase has come to an end.

Crosscutting can also form parallels by showing a line of action that happens in several different geographical locations at the same time. For instance, *That Darn Cat!* (Robert Stevenson, 1965), a chase comedy featuring a cat, uses crosscutting with different geographical locations in a hilarious manner. DC, a cat belonging to a young woman, witnesses a kidnapping

Robie (Cary Grant) and Francie (Grace Kelly) in a
speeding sports car.

Thwarted, the police give up their chase of Robie and Francie.

during his evening walk. The FBI sets up headquarters in the young woman's bedroom, and the supervisor takes up his post there, relaying orders to his agents by radio.

The agents, with their faces serious and intent, follow DC from a side street to a backyard, a butcher shop to a garbage bin. The scene crosscuts between the activity of the FBI supervisor and his agents, creating a dichotomy between the two actions: one group statically waiting in one room and another actively chasing a cat. (The editing between the agents and DC is also crosscutting, as it happens.)

After a long scene of parallel editing between the woman's bedroom and the nighttime streets, DC appears to go into the den of the kidnappers at last. *Eureka!* The FBI agents break into a room from an emergency exit and find themselves in . . . the young woman's bedroom. Meanwhile, DC has just finished his regular evening walk and returned home. The woman and the FBI supervisor, who is still instructing his men by radio, are both astonished when the separate geographical locations that have been shown by crosscutting are connected all of a sudden. As such, the contrast created by crosscutting formulates suspense and climactic emotional effects.

## Editing of the Gaze: Point of View

The chases in Hitchcock films are particularly exciting because another editing technique, known as "POV (point of view) editing," is exquisitely combined with crosscutting. In POV editing, a shot is taken from a camera that is placed at the height of a character's eyes. A close-up or a medium shot of the character looking at something off-screen is placed before and/or after the first shot. This creates the sense that we the viewers are seeing what the character is looking at.

A good example of this occurs in *The Private Life of a Cat,* a 1944 short film by experimental filmmakers Alexander Hammid and Maya Deren; in it, we see the points of view of cats that live in an apartment in Greenwich Village through the technique of POV editing. Without the use of human actors, *The Private Life of a Cat* tells of a love story between an orange cat and a white cat—their first meeting, mating, and the birth of their young. Through POV editing, we see, for example, the father cat watching his children climbing up to higher ground and playing around. We the viewers connect our viewpoint to the father cat's and warmly watch those kittens. *I Am a Cat* (*Wagahai wa neko dearu*), the 1975 Japanese film based on a famous novel by Natsume Sōseki and directed by Ichikawa Kon, is similarly full of POV editing from a cat's viewpoint. For instance, the visit of the wife of a nouveau riche to the protagonist's house is seen by a cat through a shoji window. The cat's viewpoint emphasizes that the woman is an uninvited guest.

A number of examples of POV editing can be found in *To Catch a Thief.* As a result, we feel that someone is always looking at someone else, or that somebody is always being looked at by somebody else. That is, *To Catch a Thief* is a film that explores how the humans gaze follows (chases) other humans, too.

For example, in one scene, Robie is standing in a hotel lobby. What follows is a long shot of Francie posing like a fashion model. She wears an elegant bathing suit that no one has ever seen before; the suit was designed for this film by Edith Head, a leading Hollywood designer who received eight Oscars. Grace Kelly was Edith Head's favorite actress, and, according to film historian James M. Vest, they did a fashion tour together in Paris right before the production of the film began (Vest 2003, 61). Grace Kelly was in fact a perfect fashion model for Edith Head. Her role in *Rear Window* (1954), Hitchcock's previous film, was that of a fashion model.

The shots of Robie looking and Francie posing appear by turn. As a result, we the viewers feel that Robie is looking at Francie. This is how POV editing works. In reality, however, these two shots might have been taken at a different set at different times. However, we the viewers do not usually think that way. Rather, we follow Robie's gaze, connect our viewpoint to his, see the woman in a beautiful bathing suit, and are enchanted. If Robie looks a little agitated, then we cannot help sympathizing with his shock at unexpectedly seeing a woman in such sexy clothes.

What we should also note here is that the POV editing is used to enhance the gendered gaze. While the issues of gender and sexuality will be

Robie shifts his gaze in a hotel lobby.

Francie poses like a fashion model.

elaborated on in the following chapter, it is still noteworthy to briefly introduce theories of the gendered gaze in cinema here. The term "gaze" was
first popularized in the 1960s by psychoanalyst Jacques Lacan to describe the
anxious state that occurs when one becomes aware that she or he is viewed
and feels that she or he loses autonomy and turns into an object (Lacan 1978,
73–75). Also in the 1960s, French philosopher Michel Foucault started using
the term "gaze" in his book *The Birth of the Clinic: An Archeology of Medical
Perception* (1963) and then in the 1970s in *Discipline and Punish: The Birth of
the Prison* (1977) to point out power dynamics and disciplinary mechanisms
between doctors and patients, teachers and pupils, and prison guards and
prisoners (see, for instance, Foucault 1963, 114; Foucault 1977, 205).

With such psychoanalytic and historical contexts behind the term
"gaze" in mind, in the 1970s, along with the development in feminist movements, film theorist Laura Mulvey introduced the concept of the "male gaze"
and pointed out that mainstream films, particularly Hollywood films, naturalize conventional gender relations where the figure of woman functions as
the object of male desire. In her influential 1975 essay "Visual Pleasure and
Narrative Cinema," Mulvey argued that the fascination of Hollywood films
was based on the desire to see (she uses the Freudian term "scopophilia" to
describe this desire). According to Mulvey, the POV editing, in particular,
subsumed the gaze of the camera into that of the (usually heterosexual male)
protagonist and then aligned the gaze with that of the spectator.

Three levels of the gaze (camera, male protagonist, and spectator) are
connected here. The first gaze (looking at another character, often female)
produces voyeuristic pleasure, whereas the second gaze (identification with
the character) creates narcissistic visual pleasure. Mulvey attacked mainstream cinema by claiming that this system of gaze assumed the spectator's
identification with the desiring (or powerful) protagonist who turned the
female character into a passive (or powerless) object.

In the bathing suit scene in *To Catch a Thief,* which I referred to above,
Francie is clearly displayed as a voyeuristic object of Robie's male gaze. But at
the same time, Robie also becomes an object of the gaze. In such cases, Robie
is treated either as a visual pleasure for the "female gaze" or as an anxious and
rather vulnerable object, and the system of gendered gaze is maintained in a
little more complex manner. Following Mulvey, a number of critics including
Steve Neale have pointed out that there are numerous instances of the male
body functioning as the object of gaze in mainstream films (Neale 1983,
2–17). Those examples illustrate that the gendered gaze is also applicable to
male objectification, that the gaze is not essentially male, and that there can
be contradictions in apparently normative systems of gender relations.

More importantly, in this particular scene, Francie knows full well that Robie is looking at her. Her over-the-top swimsuit and her hyperbolic sensual pose even make us the viewers aware of the objectifying male gaze. That is probably why Robie looks embarrassed rather than delighted. If that is the case, the apparent relationship between the viewer and the viewed is reversed. Robie is not really the active owner of the gaze but the actual object of the chase. Francie is not the passive object of the gaze, but she may be the leader of the chase. Thus, we can say that the POV editing in this scene is used not in a literary but in a critical or twisted manner. We will discuss the issues of self-awareness in the gendered gaze and performance of gender (feminine masquerade, etc.) in detail in the following chapter.

## The Cat and the Police

Now let's look at how effectively POV editing is used in *To Catch a Thief* to turn chases into gazes. First of all, there is a chase between The Cat and the police. Here, Robie turns into a rather vulnerable-looking object at first. However, in the end, it becomes clear that he is not simply an object of gaze. Robie's strategy is to confuse the officers by making use of the fact that he is always watched by them. The key, for Robie, is to keep watching them while knowing that he is being watched. As a result, it is always Robie who wins the chase.

The first chase occurs when the police visit Robie's house for the first time. Robie is gardening and his black cat is taking a nap on a sofa. Both of them hear screeching tires and turn their gazes in that direction. A police car is climbing up the steep hill in an extreme long shot.

Robie turns his gaze.

Robie's cat turns his gaze.

A police car is climbing up the hill.

Robie goes inside the house right away. Calling his maid, he runs up to his bedroom on the second floor and looks out a window. Four plainclothes detectives get out of the car and arrive at the gate. Robie turns his eyes to a porch, but a detective already stands there. Every time Robie turns his gaze, the shot that follows shows detectives. With POV editing, each officer appears in turn as the one that is seen by Robie (and his black cat).

Robie can only go back down to the living room and welcome the detectives. He asks them if he can change to formal attire before he goes to the police station with them, then goes back into his bedroom and closes the door. As soon as Robie vanishes from the screen, it seems as though the one who watches and the one who is watched switch places. Now it is the detectives who are looking at the closed door of the bedroom. Suddenly, a gunshot is heard from behind the door. The detectives rush over and break into the room. The following shot shows a rifle, an upturned chair, and an empty room. The detectives look at them, and we see an example here of POV editing. Then we hear, from outside of a window, the sound of a car leaving. Rushing out and getting back into the police car, the detectives follow a red sports car that has just driven away.

A car chase begins in front of the graceful mountains of Provence. But when the sports car is forced to stop by a group of sheep, the detectives find that it is not Robie but his maid who has driven the car. Realizing they've been tricked, the detectives make a U-turn and head back to Robie's house. In front of the house, Robie is calmly waiting for a bus. When the bus arrives, he climbs aboard, looks out the window, and sees that the police car has just come back. POV editing is used again. It is Robie who is now

The detectives break into Robie's room.

A rifle and an upturned chair are left in Robie's room.

the watcher. In fact, he has been in that position from the beginning of this scene until the end. He is the first winner of this chase.

This is exactly what cats do in their chases: they pretend to switch sides from being the watcher to the watched. In fact, they never stop watching and are always conscious of being watched. My cat knows that she is being watched and consciously treats me coldly and hides behind something in order to attract my attention. When I start chasing her, she joyfully runs away. When I think she has gone far away and stop chasing her, she is back before I know it and waits for me to catch up. Then, the chase starts again. I'm always the one who falls for her strategy. She always catches me.

With a feeling of victory, Robie smiles and takes a seat at the back of the bus. But when he looks to one side, he finds two birds hysterically chasing each other in a birdcage. On his other side sits Hitchcock himself

Robie looks out of a bus window.

The police car comes back. Note how Robie's face is reflected in the bus window.

Hitchcock—*The real chase has not yet begun.*

wearing a serious expression. It is as though he is warning Robie, and us, that it is too early to feel secure, that the real chase has not yet begun.

In the scene at a masquerade ball, which is the climax of the film, Robie adopts this strategy once more to confuse the watchful gaze of the police. Guests arrive one after another wearing luxurious jewelry and costumes from the period of Louis XV. POV editing emphasizes that they are objects of the gaze of the watching police, who are awaiting the right time to arrest The Cat. Francie, Mrs. Stevens, and Robie, in a costume with a black mask, are all being watched by the police. But Robie skillfully switches his costume with someone else's when he pretends to go back to a room to bring Mrs. Stevens her medication. Failing to notice the switch, the police officers do not move their gazes away from Francie and the man with the black mask, who continue their dance until the very end of the party. POV editing continues. The police are always the watchers. But nothing dramatic happens on the dance floor. At this point a close-up of Robie appears. Standing in the dark on the roof, he has been looking at everyone and everything at the party. Pretending to be watched, Robie has in fact always been the watcher. It is not only the police who are tricked by the chase of gazes. Without knowing that the real Cat is watching, the false Cat finally emerges.

## The Cat and "the New Kitten"

Yet, it gradually becomes clear that the chases with the police and with the false Cat are not what is most important to Robie. There is another chase happening simultaneously. Francie tempts him with sensual wordplay: "How about a new kitten?" This chase will have a greater impact on Robie's life as a free man. POV editing in this chase engages with the notion of gendered gaze in a more critical manner.

When he becomes a suspect in the robberies, Robie crafts a plan to attract and capture a rich person and use him/her as bait for the false Cat. Mrs. Stevens becomes Robie's target. He uses the same tactics with her as he used with the police: he pretends to be watched by her but in fact watches her. Robie appears three times in front of Mrs. Stevens, who spends a graceful evening at a luxury hotel. POV editing is used each time to make Robie an object of Mrs. Stevens' gaze. The first time is in the dining room, where Robie is a young bachelor who dines alone. The second time is in the hotel lobby, where he is a rich man discussing imitation jewels with a concierge. The third time is at a roulette table in the casino, where he is a comical character who accidentally drops a chip down a lady's dress. Mrs. Stevens looks at him on each occasion. She cannot help laughing at him and eventually invites him for a drink. Robie's tactics, or his performance to become an object of her gaze, have worked well.

Robie dines and leaves the restaurant alone.

Robie discusses imitation jewels.

Robie drops a chip down a lady's dress.

Mrs. Stevens looks at Robie on each occasion.

But Robie has misjudged one thing. Mrs. Stevens has a clever "kitten," whose name is Francie. Robie keeps winning the chases with the police and Mrs. Stevens by maintaining his position as the watcher while he pretends to be watched. But he cannot easily have his own way when it comes to Francie. This is because Francie adopts the same strategy as Robie. She makes the one whom she chases chase her, without letting him know that she is chasing him. She is the one who watches but pretends not to. This is what is going on in the hotel lobby when she puts on the elegant bathing suit in the scene that we examined earlier. Apparently, Francie is an object of gendered gaze; the POV editing of the scene emphasizes that. However, in reality, it is Robie who is targeted as the game of the chase. He is the object of Francie's gaze, a dynamic that is not explicitly displayed in the POV editing. The POV editing and the system of gendered gaze are deliberately used in a deceptive manner.

Robie is unaware of being gazed at by Francie.

In fact, Robie has already lost the first chase of gazes with Francie without even knowing it. Robie takes a brief rest at the beach in front of a luxurious hotel after his first victory over the police. Being fully satisfied, he is completely unaware of a gaze trained on him from behind. There is a mysterious woman in a yellow bathing suit with big sunglasses. It is Francie. POV editing is not used here, and in fact Hitchcock may have carefully avoided using POV editing from Francie's position in order to emphasize this irony: without a doubt, there is a relationship between the watcher and the watched. The former is Francie and the latter is Robie.

## A Truth Born Out of a Lie: Intellectual Montage

Francie's operation reaches a climax in a night of fireworks. The love scene between Robie and Francie at a hotel room is over the top and even makes us laugh. But the more hyperbolic the situation becomes, the more strongly we can feel the true emotions that they are trying to hide from each other. This coexistence of artificiality and truthfulness is craftily expressed by the third editing technique that appears in this film: "intellectual montage."

Intellectual montage is an editing technique that combines two shots with different images that do not have any obvious connection. Their collision brings about new meanings, complex concepts, or even subjective messages that cannot be expressed by each individual image. Soviet filmmaker Sergei Eisenstein came up with this idea of intellectual montage while examining hieroglyphs and Chinese and Japanese languages and characters. For instance, the collision of the characters "eye" and "water" produces the concept "crying" (Eisenstein 1998, 82–92). Three shots of lion statues (not domestic cats but the same family) in Eisenstein's *Battleship Potemkin* (1925) are a typical example of intellectual montage. The Cossack troops of the Russian Empire massacre civilians on the Odessa Steps. The sailors of the *Battleship Potemkin* revolt against the oppression and start to fire the cannons at the Cossack troops on the Steps. Between a shot of the firing cannons and that of a collapsing building, three shots are inserted: a statue of a sleeping lion, that of a lion awake, and that of a lion standing up and roaring. There is no specific connection between the sailors and the lion statues. However, when they are shown one after another, a new meaning emerges. It is as if civilians, who are strong by nature but have been silent, have finally awakened and stood up.

Intellectual montage is only one element of Soviet montage theory, which explores cinema that relies upon editing to create complex ideological and intellectual concepts and ideas from connected images. The editing methods of Soviet montage theory include metric (based purely on the specific

The lion is asleep

The lion is awake.

And the lion stands up roaring.

number of frames), rhythmic (based on a compositional relationship between shots), tonal (based on the emotional reactions of viewers), vertical (focused on non visual elements in shots), and more. Eisenstein considered intellectual montage, in particular, to be an alternative method of editing to the so-called "continuity editing" of the mainstream Hollywood cinema. Filmmaker D. W. Griffith, "the father of Hollywood cinema," developed continuity editing in the 1910s with the goal of creating a universal language of cinema for audiences of all classes all over the world. The editing techniques that we have discussed so far—the 180-degree rule, crosscutting, and POV editing—are representatives of continuity editing. The focus of continuity editing is to formulate a smooth and seamless narrative development for viewers. This can be achieved by consistency of time and physical location between shots. As long as a logical progression of shots is established, the narrative is clearly intelligible. The viewers do not even notice the cuts between shots as long as the combination of images makes visual sense. In contrast, montage, as formulated by Eisenstein, is "an idea that derives from the collision between two shots that are independent of one another" (Eisenstein 1998, 95).

Let's go back to the hotel room, where Robie and Francie stand by the windows. Fireworks have begun outside. Turning off the light, Francie says to Robie, "If you want to see the fireworks, it's better with the lights out. You're going to see one of the Riviera's most fascinating sights." Robie is taken aback at her enticing words. Even in the darkened room, Francie is given three-point lighting. Her body in a strapless white dress, her breast with diamond necklaces, and her platinum blonde hair are all shining. Here, a shot of fireworks is inserted. Then, in the following shot, Francie says seductively from a sofa where she lies, "Look, John. Hold them. Diamonds, the only thing in the world you can't resist." This is followed by a shot of fireworks that have become brighter. Simultaneously, the violin score becomes louder.

Francie kisses Robie's fingers and places his hand on her diamond necklace. She comes closer and says, "Ever had a better offer in your whole life? One with everything?" Does she mean her diamonds or herself? These explicitly sensual lines make us embarrassed and may even provoke laughter. A shot of fireworks is inserted for the third time; they have suddenly become very showy. In the following shot, the camera starts to move erratically and shows a close-up of Robie's face and then turns to that of Francie. Then appears an extremely bright shot of fireworks. The duration of each shot becomes shorter and shorter.

As if telling himself that both diamonds and Francie's offer are false, Robie says, "You know as well as I do this necklace is imitation." But Francie replies, "Well, I'm not." Robie cannot help kissing her. The next shot is filled with fireworks. The screen is almost all white. The violin score is at a climax, too. The camera comes closer and closer to the couple kissing on the sofa. Then comes an explosive shot of fireworks.

"Look, John. Hold them."

Fireworks begin.

"I'm not imitation."

Fireworks explode.

While Robie and Francie are kissing in the hotel room, the fireworks are reaching their climax outside of the room. In that sense, this editing is a variation of crosscutting. Unlike the chase scenes, however, even if all the shots of the fireworks are omitted, viewers will never lose track of the smooth progression of the storyline. There is something else behind the editing here, and that is intellectual montage. When the shots of fireworks, which become brighter and fiercer, are combined with those of Robie and Francie, who come closer and closer, the collision of images creates a new idea. In other words, we the viewers, who have been paying attention to the screen, try to read new meanings and emotions into the combination of shots. For instance, we may think that even though Robie and Francie pretend to be cool, they have fierce romantic feelings inside and their passions for each other are heightening in this scene, or something of the sort. We think that the fireworks are a metaphor for their emotional states. The images of the couple and the fireworks collide and thus are forcefully connected. Film scholar Lesley Brill makes the following argument about the scene:

> This foolishness charms us partly because its self-conscious excesses are impossible to take seriously. The most familiar aural and visual clichés of cinematic courtship—violins, fireworks, divinely glamorous protagonists—are sent up together in an *inflatio ad absurdum*. Behind the amorous folly, however, uninsistent but unconcealed, Hitchcock makes his straightforward point: this is all make-believe, as unreal as it is overstated. "You know as well as I do they're fake," says John about Francie's diamonds. The emotion is fake, too, "weird excitement," not love. (Brill 1988, 38)

However, such a forged connection of independent images by intellectual montage comes to express the true emotions of the entangled couple, no matter how strongly they try to make their emotions appear fake. It is a truth born out of a lie, so to speak. Hitchcock once said that emotions could be created by editing so that actors need not do anything but be there. What he has resorted to here is intellectual montage.

According to the original screenplay of *To Catch a Thief*, in addition to the fireworks, a shot of a cat walking toward the camera until it fully covers the entire screen was supposed to be inserted into this love scene. Again, there is no innate connection between a cat and the couple. But if this shot of a cat had been connected to the shots of the couple, we the viewers would most likely have started to think of new meanings—perhaps the cat is about to attack someone or catch some person or valuable jewel, or some such thing. But who catches whom? The cat is a metaphor for whom? Is it Robie, or Francie?

## Uh-oh—The Cat Is Caught

In the end, Robie catches the false Cat and proves his innocence. He appears to regain his freedom. But it looks as though he has lost the chase with a young woman. When he is about to relax at his house on the hill, he is surprised by an intruder. Previously, when the police came, he immediately placed himself in the position of a viewer. He was prepared for the chase with them. But he fails this time. Francie appears on the veranda out of the blue. She clings to his shoulder and murmurs sweetly, "So this is where you live. Mother will love it up here!" Robie is flabbergasted, but it is too late.

The chapel bells ring in benediction as though celebrating a marriage. The film comes to an end.

Hitchcock called this an almost tragic ending. It is Francie who wins the chase. Just like that, the Cat is caught.

## Author's note:

Jessie Royce Landis, who plays Mrs. Stevens, Francie's mother, played the role of Cary Grant's mother in *North by Northwest* (1959), the next Hitchcock film in which Grant would appear. Could this be a joke? Hitchcock's way of carrying the story beyond one film?

# PART II

# Theories and Histories of Cinema

# CHAPTER 4

# Cats Are Prima Donnas

## Feminist Film Theory and Auteurism in *Dishonored*

*Josef von Sternberg, USA, 1931*

### Dietrich Is a Cat, Too

Like Audrey Hepburn in *Breakfast at Tiffany's,* Simone Simon in *Cat People,* and Cary Grant in *To Catch a Thief,* Marlene Dietrich in *Dishonored* is a cat-like character. *Dishonored* is a tragic love story set in Vienna during World War I. The Austrian spy X27, played by Dietrich, is cat-like from beginning to end. A nameless cat is always with X27: on her bed, on the piano with which X27 plays "Waves of the Danube (Valurile Dunarii)," on her lap when she rides in a biplane to steal into enemy territory, and in jail after she is sentenced to death for treason. At times, it seems as if X27 is a black Persian cat and the real body in a human shape next to it is only its imitator.

The film opens with a close-up of a street lamp illuminating a rainy night. Under the lamp, a woman wearing a coat with a black fur collar and cuffs raises her skirt a little and fixes her stockings and garter belt. Her legs, slightly peeping out from the skirt, are shown in a close-up and shine white under the streetlight. This is ostensibly an erotic image. But the owner of these legs seems to be aware that somebody is watching her and is consciously showing off her beautiful legs. We sense this because the way she fixes her stockings is somewhat pretentious, perhaps even unnecessary. We the viewers sense that she is a prostitute performing an erotic move. Her action also reminds us of a cat cleaning its wet legs. Cats do not like to get wet. Cary Grant in *To Catch a Thief* also tends to his wet sleeve so much when he escapes by boat that he is teased by Danielle, a young French woman: "Cats don't like water."

A woman fixes her stockings under a street lamp:
Close-up of her legs.

Medium shot of the woman's face (Marlene Dietrich).

In the shot that follows, the woman turns her face halfway to the camera
as if she were seducing someone. Her face is covered by a black veil, but her
eyes shine from the reflected streetlight, just as the eyes of a cat often glow
in the dark. What she looks at with her radiant eyes is a building across the
street. A crowd has gathered there while policemen and emergency rescue
team members go in and out of the building. She holds her stare and slowly
comes closer to the camera while placing one of her hands on her hip. Here

it becomes clear to us, the viewers, that this woman is played by Dietrich. Of course, many viewers might have recognized this with the first close-up of Dietrich adjusting her garter belt because she was already famous for her beautiful legs.

Someone is carried into an emergency vehicle on a stretcher. It seems that a young prostitute has committed suicide. Among the people on the side street, there are apparently other women of the same occupation as well as a gentleman with a fine mustache, possibly a customer of one of the women. The woman played by Dietrich looks at the situation and says to no one in particular, "I'm not afraid of life. Although I am not afraid of death, either." The gentleman with the mustache hears this and speaks to her.

There are two things that we should pay particular attention to in this opening scene. First, the prostitute played by Dietrich is clearly depicted as an erotic object. It looks as though she is consciously performing in an erotic way. Second, POV editing (see the previous chapter) emphasizes her gaze. In other words, this opening scene indicates that the prostitute that Dietrich plays is an object of male desire yet she is simultaneously a subject who firmly looks back at a society controlled by men.

When the prostitute invites the gentleman into her room as the night's guest, her body is placed under a big dark shadow that the man and his umbrella create. Visually, it looks as though she is captured under his big wing. Yet, at the same time, she keeps staring at him. The man, by contrast, does not turn his eyes to her, as if she were too vulgar for him. He only spits out, "I need a woman who knows how to deal with men."

As soon as she hears this, the prostitute starts to take conspicuously sensual poses. His comment sounds like a sexual innuendo, but his facial expression indicates that this gentleman is not very interested in the prostitute sexually; rather, he appears to be recruiting her, to turn her into a terrorist or something similar. With wine glasses in her hand, she responds, "It's against Austria, of course."

"Of course," says the man.

"I'd like to get some wine," she replies. When she comes back after a few seconds, what she brings back with her is not a bottle of wine but a policeman who has been patrolling nearby. She accuses the gentleman of being an anti-Austrian spy. Thus, it is the prostitute who captures the man using her gaze while she performs as an erotic object.

Even though the prostitute has made a nihilistic remark in the opening scene ("I'm not afraid of life. Although I am not afraid of death, either"), she is not antisocial or rebellious toward her own country. In fact, the prostitute obediently responds to a police summons on the following morning. It is the gentleman with the mustache who awaits her at the police station. He was not arrested the night before. He is the head of the Austrian Secret Service and was testing her patriotism. Respecting her model action the previous evening, he asks her to work as a spy for Austria. Without any hesitation, she agrees.

But both the secret service head and we the viewers cannot help but feel a little uneasy. Isn't she a little too obedient? Isn't she too pretentious? When she arrives at the police station, when she is guided through a corridor by a young officer, when she listens to the head's story in front of a blind that makes numerous lines of shadow, and when she leans into a chair and agrees to become a spy, the prostitute in the black coat keeps playing with the fur of her coat or casting meaningful glances. Her behaviors look like those of a cat posing and playing a prima donna. She is not rebellious. She does not take any antisocial actions. She apparently has an attitude that makes her customers happy. Still, her attitude seems ostentatious. It looks like a performance. Her real intention is hidden from the head as well as the viewers.

Similarly, on the previous evening, after she hands over the mustachioed gentleman to the patrolman she approaches the camera and vigorously starts to play the piano that sits in her apartment. Her Persian cat sits next to the piano. The prostitute is so close to the camera that her face protrudes from the frame (an extreme close-up). Yet, even from such a close distance, her expression is inscrutable. We cannot really figure out what she thinks or how she feels.

The woman plays the piano in an extreme close-up.

## Dietrich and Feminist Film Theory

As we have seen in the previous chapter, film theorist Laura Mulvey claimed in "Visual Pleasure and Narrative Cinema" that Hollywood films cater to the desiring male gaze, which turns female characters into passive objects of voyeuristic pleasure. For Mulvey, Josef von Sternberg's films were "fetishistic scopophilia" and Hitchcock's were "sadistic" voyeurism that supported the patriarchal gender hierarchy (Mulvey 1999, 840). Dietrich was, according to Mulvey, "a perfect product, whose body, stylized and fragmented by close-ups, is the content of the film and the direct recipient of the spectator's look" (Mulvey 1999, 841).

However, Dietrich's character seems to go beyond being a passive object of male gaze. Film theorist E. Ann Kaplan argues that Dietrich deliberately uses her body as spectacle (Kaplan 1983, 51). Gaylyn Studlar, another film theorist, suggests that in Sternberg's films Dietrich is also empowered and entraps male characters with her charms while she offers voyeuristic pleasure to the male gaze (Studlar 1988, 243). Dietrich's own gaze undermines the sense that the male gaze is always active and powerful. Studlar thus regards Dietrich as a dialectic figure who is both the passive object and the gaze's perpetrator.

I want to build on the views of Kaplan and Studlar and more recent feminist theory with my own feminist reading of *Dishonored*, which emphasizes the notion of performance. In her influential book *Gender Trouble: Feminism and the Subversion of Identity*, feminist philosopher Judith Butler proposes the idea of gender performance. According to Butler, our gender is constructed through our own repetitive performance of gender (Butler 1990, 95). Such repetition is forced by "oppressive and painful gender norms," argues Butler (Butler and Kotz 1992, 84). What Dietrich's character does in this film is to perform her femininity by using men as the ones who force her into what she is. X27 does not passively accept her position as an object for erotic male gazes; rather, she is aware that her body is a commodity, or a pet, and consciously performs the role of a sexually and socially weak figure. She does so in such an overtly erotic manner that even pleasure-seeking male viewers often feel uncomfortable. By doing so, her performance highlights the unequal and oppressive social structure that has deprived her of her husband and turned her into a prostitute for society men and governmental officials. She does not publicly oppose her country. She does not become an antisocial terrorist. Were she to do so, she would most likely be oppressed again. A more effective strategy is to appear to maintain the sexual and social power structure on the surface but cast doubt on it by her exaggerated mannerisms.

As a result of X27's performance, uneasy feelings stir among governmental officials. The power structure has not been reversed but is shaken up. It becomes unclear who really controls the situation. Film scholar Andrea Weiss even argues that Dietrich's sexual ambiguity, the result of a "masculinization" of her characters, was embraced by gay and lesbian audiences (Weiss 1992, 42). *Entertainment Weekly* chose Taylor Swift as the 2010 Entertainer of the Year and put her on the cover of its December issue. In the photo, Swift wears a tuxedo, a white bow tie, and a silk hat. This costume is exactly what Dietrich wore in *Morocco* (Sternberg, 1930) and proves that Dietrich's image still appeals to a broad audience.

The historical context behind such overt eroticization of Dietrich in her films was the financial situation of the production company where she worked. Dietrich played a mysterious cabaret singer in *Morocco*, charming prostitutes in *Dishonored* and *Shanghai Express* (Sternberg 1932), and a chaste wife/mother who becomes a cabaret dancer in *Blonde Venus* (Sternberg 1932). All of these films were produced and released by Paramount, which was facing bankruptcy, before the enforcement of the Production Code in 1934. The Hollywood film industry was increasingly sensitive about sex, and it was a high-risk gamble to let a star play the explicitly sexy roles of a dancer or a prostitute. In fact, during the production of *Blonde Venus,* the screenplay and the prints were checked several times. Yet, Paramount was gambling on exactly these types of sexy star vehicles in addition to trying to reduce production costs (Baxter 1993, 39–84). It was helpful that Dietrich was an exotic star who had just arrived from Germany and already had an image as a sex symbol. Even if she was depicted as bold and sexy, it was excusable because she was not an American.

### Feigning a Harmless Kitten: Performance and Masquerade

*Dishonored* is indeed a film about performance. X27 changes her costumes one after another and gives numerous performances in different disguises. With her performances, she succeeds in a number of important missions.

First Act: X27's first mission is to steal into a masquerade ball, seduce Colonel von Hindau (Warner Orlando, who was famous for playing Charlie Chan, a Chinese detective), a suspected betrayer, and seize evidence of his betrayal. X27 puts on a mask that looks like a vulture or a cat, a shiny black mini-dress that hugs her body, and a cape that reminds us of a gladiator's. She finds Hindau, who wears the costume of a hangman, right away (POV editing) and openly begins a performance of temptation. She sends a sensual gaze to him from behind her mask, exhibits some sort of courtship

X27 seduces Hindau (Warner Orlando).

behavior with a party toy, allows her leg to show from under the hem of her mini-dress, and smokes a cigarette in a seductive manner. But when he is not watching her, she looks around carefully with a serious expression, extends her arm like a cat to the back of a painting on the wall, and looks for evidence.

Second Act: Her next mission is to infiltrate a hotel in Russia, seduce a Russian officer, and steal military secrets. This time, X27 wears the far-from-fancy dress of a maid. When I watched this film for the first time as an undergraduate, I didn't recognize the maid as Dietrich in disguise for some time. She has her eye on one officer as she begins her performance as a naïve innocent. When he looks at her legs, she opens her eyes wide and bashfully hides her face with her skirt. She then climbs up to the top of a cupboard and innocently imitates a cat's meow in order to draw his attention. When he drinks too much and passes out, she starts to copy the secret military documents he keeps. On her way out, however, she is captured by Colonel Kranau (Victor McLaglen), an enemy spy. She does not give up easily. When he turns his back on her, she opens her eyes wide like a cat in the dark and glances right and left to look for an escape route. As she does this, she holds her Persian cat right next to her face. Her cat also glances around exactly as X27 does.

Kranau triumphantly says, "Everybody makes mistakes. And you carry a cat." When X27 replies, "It has brought me good luck, so far," he asks her, "Do you call this good luck?" X27 answers, "I don't know yet." In front

X27 and her cat glance around.

of a mirror, she arranges her maid's dress to look a little bit sexy. Then, she slowly clings to Kranau. Thus she resets her disguise and performance. It will not take long for Kranau to relax his guard and drink wine containing a sleeping drug. In the end, X27 escapes from Russia, returns safely to Vienna, and delivers the military information to her boss.

Third and Final Act: Even facing her own execution, she keeps up her performance. She asks, "Could you possibly help me to die in a uniform of my own choosing?" What she puts on for her final act is the black fur-trimmed coat of a prostitute that she wore when the film began: "[A] dress I wore when I served my countrymen instead of my country," according to her. Using the young officer's saber as a mirror, she puts on lipstick. Then she sticks her left hand in a pocket, straightens herself up in the exaggerated manner of a prostitute, and starts to walk. It looks as though she has started her final performance.

The young officer is moved by her attitude and loses sight of his duty. The moment the shooting corps point their guns at X27 and X27 makes an exaggerated sign of the cross with her right hand, he cries out. "I will not kill a woman. I will not kill any more men, either. Do you call this war? I call it butchery! You call this serving your country? You call this patriotism? I call it murder!" The young officer is held down and taken out by other soldiers. In the meantime, X27 fixes her lips again. Unlike the young officer, she does not overtly revolt against her country. Instead, she chooses to improve her performance and disguise with her lipstick. As she did at the beginning of

X27 fixes her lips before being executed.

the film, she raises her skirt, shows off her beautiful legs, and fixes her stockings. When she is shot, she swings up her arms and falls down on her back. This is a typical performance of death by a stage actor. Thus, she never stops acting up to the moment of her death.

X27 does not have the power to change her fate. She knows that her life is predetermined by the patriarchal system of power and desire and is conscious of how such a system wants her to behave. She chooses to continuously perform the ideal role of a woman that the system requires. She puts on a mask of femininity as a masquerade. By doing so in an overt manner, she makes those empowered by it realize how the system is working. They end up feeling discomfort and guilt because of such exposure. This is her method of resistance. Here, it is worthwhile to refer to the notion of masquerade that feminist film theorist Mary Ann Doane explores, drawing on the work of British psychoanalyst Joan Rivière. Rivière claimed in her 1929 essay "Womanliness as a Masquerade" that women who found themselves in a male position of authority put on a mask of femininity that would function as compensation for their masculine position. They would overemphasize their feminine characteristics and appearances. Doane resorts to this notion of masquerade when she argues that female spectators who must identify with the male gaze when they watch Hollywood cinema can wear a mask of femininity for compensation (Doane 1982, 81–84). Doane claims, "The masquerade doubles representation; it is constituted by a hyperbolisation of the accoutrements of femininity" (Doane 1982, 82). Consciously wearing

X27 plays the "Moonlight Sonata" with a tender expression on her face, which is reflected in the cover of the piano.

the mask of femininity, or an excess of femininity, as a masquerade, X27 reveals the apparent normative system of gendered gaze.

There are at least two scenes in the film in which X27 displays a tender expression and looks off into the distance. It is noteworthy that in both scenes she is alone. What she thinks and feels remains ambiguous, but her facial expression is clearly different from that she has worn in other scenes. Framing and lighting enhance this difference.

X27 exhibits this expression for the first time when she plays the "Moonlight Sonata" by Beethoven on the grand piano in her room right after she has met Kranau for the first time. Her tender expression is reflected on the cover of the piano on which she plays the passionate but yearning tune, making it seem as if she were torn in two. Is this a metaphor for her feelings towards Kranau that she tries so hard to hide?

The second time is when she looks outside, where a number of searchlights brighten the evening sky to search for Kranau. Right before this shot, X27 has volunteered to question Kranau, who has been arrested by the border police. During the investigation, whether intentionally or not, she drops her gun and lets him escape. This is why she is sentenced to death for treason. Even though X27 stands in a dark room with all the lamps turned off, her face is lit from the front top in a close-up. Her eyes and hair shine beautifully in the light, enhancing her expression of contentment.

Dietrich in the "north light."

According to Lee Garmes, who was the cinematographer for many of Dietrich's early Hollywood films including *Dishonored,* this is the so-called "north light," the light from the top, or north, that he invented to beautifully display Dietrich's facial features. Garmes once said,

> Unfortunately I didn't have sufficient time to make tests of Marlene Dietrich; I had seen *The Blue Angel* [*Der blau Engel,* 1930, Sternberg's German film with Dietrich], and, based on that, I lit her with a sidelight, a half-tone, so that one half of her face was bright and the other half was in shadow. I looked at the first day's work and I thought, 'My God, I can't do this, it's exactly what Bill Daniels is doing with Garbo.' We couldn't, of course, have two Garbos! So, without saying anything to Jo, I changed to the north-light effect. He had no suggestions for changes, he went ahead and let me do what I wanted. The Dietrich face was my creation. (Quoted in Higham 1970, 40–41)

In addition, white eyeliner makes her shining eyes look bigger. The special lighting technique and makeup appear to emphasize X27's affection for Kranau and her satisfaction that she could save him. These two occasions of tenderness make X27's ostentatious disguises and erotic performances even more striking.

## Sternberg and Auteurism

The director and the star of *Dishonored* were just as conscious about performance as the fictional character X27. The director, Josef von Sternberg, was born in Vienna in 1894 and moved to Brooklyn, NY, when he was a child. He entered the film business in the 1910s and became a director in Hollywood during the silent era of the 1920s. When he was invited to Germany to direct *The Blue Angel* at Ufa, the largest studio in Germany, he discovered Dietrich. Returning to Hollywood, he directed a number of Dietrich star vehicles at Paramount. Those films, including *Dishonored,* paid particular attention to lighting and costume and emphasized stylistically the thematic motifs of performance and masquerade.

*The Blue Angel,* the first Sternberg–Dietrich film, is the story of a serious high school teacher falling in love with Lola-Lola, a cabaret dancer, and ruining his life. The audition for the role of Lola-Lola faced heavy going. Sternberg wanted a woman who could captivate the world. He happened to attend a theatrical play, *Zwei Krawatten,* because many supporting actors for *The Blue Angel* were in it, including Maria Magdalena Dietrich von Losch. According to Sternberg's autobiography, entitled *Fun in a Chinese Laundry,* she had heard that Sternberg was in the audience and was still looking for his Lola-Lola, but she appeared indifferent to his presence—just like a cat! Even when she came to the audition the following afternoon, she never tried to sell herself. She was no one, even after appearing in twenty-five plays and seventeen films, yet she boldly told the famous director that she doubted that he could direct women. According to Sternberg in his autobiography, "She was seated in a corner of a sofa facing my desk, her eyes downcast, a study in apathy" (Sternberg 1965, 233). Her ostentatious indifference and her "deep look of contempt" captured Sternberg's attention (Sternberg 1965, 234). He learned later that her behavior was actually a performance. According to Lee Garmes, Dietrich was conscious of the techniques of cinematography and lighting. She understood how she would be lit and photographed and thus always played roles even during auditions and interviews. Garmes claimed, "She [Dietrich] had a great mechanical mind, and knew the camera. She would always stop in the exact position that was right for her" (quoted in Higham 1970, 42).

From the very beginning, Sternberg may have known that Dietrich had been acting. He was a son of an immigrant and his family had been poor both in Vienna and in Brooklyn. Having experienced discrimination, Sternberg was extremely conscious of how he was seen by others. He himself was always acting (Baxter 1993, 87–91), and he often studied his facial expressions in front of mirrors. He was fond of having his portrait painted, his statue sculpted. He liked to display them at the parties he threw. This did not necessarily come from narcissism, for the portraits did not always depict him as handsome. He was also obsessed with costumes in his films as well as in his real life. But he was not really interested in making himself look chic, and he never followed trends. For instance, his daily clothes included a secondhand costume from a Shakespeare play. Moreover, his middle name, "von," was not his real name. He chose it when he was an assistant director because it sounded aristocratic. Also, it recalled Erich von Stroheim, an acclaimed Hollywood director who was also from Vienna, even though Stroheim was notorious for how much money he spent making his films. As such, both Sternberg's costumes and his name were a part of his performance. ("Marlene" was also a fabrication by Sternberg, by the way—the combination of Maria and Magdalena, her real name.)

Sternberg wrote, "[N]o matter how concealed the purpose of a story, it is at all times indicative of its author" (Sternberg 1965, 3). His words perfectly fit the mode of auteurism that was prevalent in film criticism when his autobiography was published in 1965.

The term *auteur* dates back to the 1920s, when French film critics and directors debated on the work of the auteur (i.e., screenplay author and filmmaker as one and the same) versus the scenario-led film (Hayward 1996, 12). In the 1950s, this debate was revived. Critics for the film journal *Cahiers du Cinéma,* including François Truffaut, Jean-Luc Godard, Claude Chabrol, and Eric Rohmer, who would all become directors, watched a number of films at the *Cinémathèque Française* in Paris and started a critical movement called auteurism (*politique des auteurs*). Auteurism was the result of a French response to a sudden influx of Hollywood films that had been held up during the German Occupation in World War II. A great number of popular and genre-based Hollywood films were examined in *Cahiers du Cinéma.*

There are four assumptions in auteurism. First, cinema is equivalent to literature, or any other art of "profundity and meaning" (Astruc 1968, 20). Second, cinema constitutes a new and unique language. Third, this situation affords directors of cinema a means of personal expression, that is, a form within which a genuine artist may "translate his obsessions" or personality (Astruc 1968, 18). Fourth, these "obsessions" can be traced through thematic and/or stylistic consistency over almost all films by the director.

In his influential 1954 essay, "A Certain Tendency in French Cinema," Truffaut made auteurism's most fundamental point: films should not be valorized by their subject matter but by paying particular attention to their use of *mise-en-scène,* or all the visual aspects that are happening on the screen

(Truffaut 1976, 234). His logic was that subject matter and screenplays were most likely under the control of studios but visual styles were likely under the control of directors. Similarly, another influential critic, André Bazin, claimed that auteurs included a "personal factor" that connected all their films together and made their work identifiable (Bazin 1985, 255). As such, in auteurism, directors who were able to impart their own styles to their films, regardless of type or narrative or the conditions under which they were made, were considered to be auteurs. Auteurism reevaluated such Hollywood filmmakers as Alfred Hitchcock and Howard Hawks, who worked in crime films, westerns, and horror films, which had been considered mass entertainment, or B-films.

Auteurism was introduced to America in 1962 largely by one person: Andrew Sarris, a film critic for the *New York Times*. While auteurism played a part in the emergence of analysis that focused on cinematic techniques instead of the stories and themes that had occupied the major areas of criticism before, Sarris admitted that auteurism was "not so much a theory as an attitude" (Caughie 1981, 65). His argument suggested that auteurism had a tendency to put too much emphasis on the director's worldview and exclude the social reality and the historical context of filmmaking as a collaborative process with the efforts of cinematographers, screenwriters, actors, etc.

In an auteurist analysis that takes Sternberg's words seriously into consideration, Sternberg's films can be read as an expression of his obsession with his star, Marlene Dietrich. For instance, in *The Devil Is a Woman* (1935), the final collaboration between Sternberg and Dietrich, declining aristocrat Don Pasquale (Lionel Atwill) tells his young rival how much he has loved Concha Pérez, the femme fatale played by Dietrich, how bitterly he has been betrayed, and how tragically he has followed the road to ruin. But at the same time, he insists that his life was happy. This apparently confident man in a spotless army uniform finds happiness in his fate even after he has suffered from humiliation and lost both his health and social status. "Were I to live my life over again I'd probably do the same foolish things once more," says Don Pasquale.

The story of Don Pasquale was an aestheticized version of Sternberg's life; he had been obsessed by Dietrich from the time he met her during the preproduction of *The Blue Angel*. Sternberg wrote in his autobiography, "She [Dietrich] has never ceased to proclaim that I taught her everything" (Sternberg 1965, 224–225). But he insisted, "Her constant praise is rated as one of her admirable virtues—by others, not by me" (Sternberg 1965, 224). He claimed that Dietrich was hiding her claws, pretending to be humble in order to be judged favorably, just as X27 consciously projected the desired

image of a woman. Still, Sternberg could not help praising Dietrich as sophisticated yet innocent, and says that he cannot believe such a beautiful woman
did not receive any attention for a long time.

## Beyond Auteurism: Collaborative Performance Between the Director and the Actor

But if both Sternberg and Dietrich were conscious of performance and masquerade, should we then consider Sternberg's overt claim about his obsession in his autobiography as well as in his films to be *his* performance? Or, to
be more exact, were they the products of the collaborative performance by
the director and the actor (and cinematographer Lee Garmes, and costume
designer Travis Banton, etc.)? Throughout the production of *The Blue Angel,*
Dietrich and Sternberg always watched the rush prints that they filmed and
then went to the editing room together. Historian Christian Esquevin argues
that Travis Banton knew that Dietrich was "no prima donna" but rather a
collaborator in the creation of her screen image. Esquevin writes,

> With Sternberg's late filming habits, Banton was forced to take
> costume fittings late in the evenings. Nevertheless, Dietrich would
> come into wardrobe late after her shooting schedule, and she
> would stand stiffly upright while Banton, the seamstresses and fit-
> ters would work, exhausted, until the early hours of the morning.
> (Esquevin 2014, n.p.)

It was even publicized from the very beginning that the ostentatiously
erotic image of Dietrich was a fabricated one. The February 1932 issue of
*Photoplay* magazine published an article on Dietrich by Kay Evans, who
wrote, "She is two different women. With von Sternberg she is what he
has made her be, the woman who wandered through 'Morocco' on a pair
of ridiculously high heels, the woman who rouged her lips before facing a
firing squad in 'Dishonored.' When she is away from him [Sternberg] she is
a gay, happy, laughing child. The mask is tossed away, the pose is gone. She is
the Marlene Dietrich of Germany and not the creation of von Sternberg of
some mystic Graustarkian country" (Evans 1932, 104).

Other magazines constantly reported that Dietrich's face when she
looked at her daughter Maria did not have the iconic cool and indifferent expression but rather the affectionate gaze of a mother. Since Dietrich
had a dual image of bold actor and reliable mother, Paramount was able to
release films that emphasized her eroticism. Yet, even this image of Dietrich's

real life might have been a performance. We cannot naively believe stars' "confessions" in fan magazines. We know that they are also part publicity and, as such, this is one area that is lacking in auteurism: it does not fully pay attention to the role of the spectator's reading process. For the advocates of auteurism, a film is not a place for active dialogues between the screen and the spectator. As French philosopher Roland Barthes pointed out in his essay "The Death of the Author," the making of meaning lies in the relationship between the text and its reader (Barthes 1977, 62). Another French philosopher, Michel Foucault, also suggests that the author ceases to be a real person and instead "performs" a classificatory function that evokes spectators' recognition and expectation (Foucault 1984, 101–120). If we follow the ideas of Barthes and Foucault that rearticulate auteurism as a theory of the social and historical subject, the auteur becomes both a person who expresses his/her "obsessions" and a performative existence with which we the viewers, whether living in the 1930s, 1950s, or today, can actively interact.

## Masquerade Forever

After all, X27's true character was not revealed until the very end. She showed tender expressions in some scenes, but only we the viewers could witness them and we could not understand what she was really thinking. X27 continued her performance until the very last moment and then departed to the other world.

The same was true of Dietrich. Together with Sternberg, Garmes, and Banton, among others, she created her image and continued her masquerade. Like X27, did she hope to reveal the power structure of the patriarchal society? The titles of Dietrich studies are filled with "images": *The Idea of the Image: Josef Von Sternberg's Dietrich Films* (1988), *Thinking in Images: Film Theory, Feminist Philosophy and Marlene Dietrich* (2006), *Dietrich Icon* (2007), and *Dressing the Part: Sternberg, Dietrich, and Costume* (1993). This fact alone is indicative of Dietrich's (and Sternberg's) life of performance.

In 1961, she published a book, *Marlene Dietrich's ABC*. In it, she explains a number of words in alphabetical order. The book is a strange mix of encyclopedia, manual, and autobiography. In the "D" section, there is an entry for "Dietrich." It reads, "In the German language: the name for a key that opens all locks. Not a magic key. A very real object, necessitating great skills in the making."

Dietrich died in 1992, so the key is lost now. The mystery behind her performance remains.

# CHAPTER 5

# Cats, Mixed and Hybrid

## Genre and Stardom in *Shozo, a Cat and Two Women*

*Toyoda Shirō, Japan, 1956*

### A Film about Cats

*Shozo, a Cat and Two Women* is a little-known but fascinating film that deserves more attention. The film is based on the novel by renowned author Tanizaki Jun'ichirō, which was originally published in 1936. The story revolves around a triangular relationship between Shōzō (Morishige Hisaya), the prodigal son of a kitchenware store owner in Ashiya, Japan, who plays around with his beloved cat, Lily, every day despite the financial trouble of his store; his wife Shinako (Yamada Isuzu), who has just decided to move out; and Fukuko (Kagawa Kyōko), the delinquent daughter of a rich relative, whom Shōzō's mother wants as his new partner.

The film was directed by Toyoda Shirō, acclaimed for turning famous literary works into cinema, including *The Wild Geese (Gan, 1953)*, based on Mori Ōgai's novel; *Snow Country (Yukiguni, 1957)*, based on Kawabata Yasunari's novel; *A Dark Night's Passing (An'ya kōro, 1959)*, based on Shiga Naoya's novel; and *The Strange Tale of Oyuki (Bokutō kidan, 1960)*, based on Nagai Kafū's novel. *Shozo, a Cat and Two Women* had legitimate success as a literary film. It was not only ranked number four in the annual "Best Ten" of *Kinema Junpō,* the most influential film journal in Japan, but also received other notable film awards in 1956. Both Miura Mitsuo, the cinematographer, and Yamada Isuzu, the leading actress, received the Blue Ribbon Award and the Mainichi Eiga Concours Award, prestigious film awards in Japan.

In this chapter, we will examine *Shozo, a Cat and Two Women* from an auteurist standpoint and discuss how the acclaimed director, Toyoda, expressed his worldview based on a famous literary work in collaboration with his crew and cast. For instance, while Tanizaki does not make any explicit connection between "a cat" and "two women" but clearly delineates them as the title of the novel indicates, the film version in numerous scenes depicts both Shinako and Fukuko as if they were cats. In Fukuko's first appearance, she is depicted exactly like a cat. Shōzō visits her room and looks for her by calling her name, as if he were playing hide and seek with a pet. Suddenly, she jumps out of a Western-style drawer and then scratches Shōzō like a cat. After spending a night with Shōzō, she stays on his futon with Lily, his cat.

Shōzō also treats Fukuko like a cat. When they go out to the beach together, he caresses her legs and arms affectionately and rubs her nose with his, exactly the same behavior that he shows to Lily at the very beginning of the film on the same beach. We can analyze Toyoda's obsession with such feline-like characters by comparing this film with others by the director, if we like. But it is more fascinating to think about *Shozo, a Cat and Two Women* from two different contexts: genre and stardom

## What Is Film Genre?

It is not really farfetched to turn to genre here in this chapter, because auteurism developed hand-in-hand with the study of film genre. Like auteurism, genre is also a French term meaning kind or class. Film critic André Bazin, one of the founders of auteurism, was particularly interested in the contexts of genre in Hollywood filmmaking. In the early 1970s, under the strong influence of auteurism, such film critics as Jim Kitses and Colin McArthur started to examine the relationship between auteurs and genres (westerns for Kitses, gangster/crime films for McArthur). That was the beginning of genre theory in cinema. Since then, various theorists have discussed the definitions of film genres, mainly based on content (themes, settings, etc.) and form (structure, style, etc.) and the usability of genres for both audiences (finding meanings and pleasures) and producers (minimizing economic risk, marketing, etc.).

Traditionally, these theorists regarded genres as fixed forms, but as film critic Daniel Chandler points out, contemporary theorists emphasize that both forms and functions of genres are dynamic (Chandler 2017, 3). A genre is not rigid or pure but fluid and hybrid—much in the same way that cats are, by the way: most cats with us today are either mixed or hybrid. One source states that about 98 percent of cats fall outside the purebred population (www.familyeducation.com/life/cats/purebred-vs-domestic-cats). Similarly, the most recent US Pet (Dog and Cat) Population Fact Sheet published by the American Humane Association, estimates that 95 percent of all US cats are "domestic shorthair," cats of mixed ancestry. Such popular breeds of cats as Savannah (with African serval) and Bengal (with Asian leopard) are hybrids with wild cats. In other words, genres (as well as cats) are constantly changing because of various factors—economic, technological, etc. Therefore, it is significant to discuss genres "as historical phenomena" (Chandler 2017, 4).

For example, everybody seems to know what "film noir" is as a genre. Neon lights. Headlights. Naked light bulbs. Streets wet with rain. Window blinds. Mirrors. Critics have tried to define it based on its content and form: themes such as memory of war, threat of communism, corruption of cities, and anxiety towards women's social participation; nightmarish visual styles such as contrasty lighting and diagonal composition; puzzling narrational styles such as flashback and voiceovers of protagonists who live in nightmarish worlds; obsessive characters such as femmes fatale and hard-boiled private eyes or police officers. The expressive lighting was influenced by German and Austrian filmmakers and technicians who fled to Hollywood from Nazi-controlled Europe in the 1930s and 1940s. Those filmmakers and technicians had experience making the so-called German Expressionist films that often depicted the anxiety and paranoia of people who lived in big cities, including criminals, detectives, and police officers, by using extremely contrasty lighting and intentionally distorted sets and the techniques of flashback and psychological point-of-view editing.

In film noir, when a character is sitting in a diner, or being questioned by the police, or is recording his confession, he may start to stare into space. After a close-up, the scene shifts to some past event in his life, and viewers realize that a flashback has begun. Thus, we the viewers start to relive a character's past from his or her viewpoint. Moreover, the flashback scenes are often accompanied by narration by the character as he or she remembers the past. This technique is called voiceover. The important thing about flashback and voiceover is that the past only exists in a character's memory: the past that they remember may not be the one that really occurred. It may only be their fantasy. Film historian Robert Sklar makes the following point about post-WWII American society: "The hallmark of *film noir* is its sense of people trapped—trapped in webs of paranoia and fear, unable to tell guilt from innocence, true identity from false" (Sklar 1994, 253).

It is clear, though, that none of those images is enough to define film noir, and it is very difficult to find films that satisfyingly include all of them. Images of film noir float around like a mirage, but never provide anything concrete enough to grasp. That's because it is a hybrid entity. The 1982 sci-fi film *Blade Runner,* directed by Ridley Scott, is one such example that explored new stylistic possibilities by combining different genres. (Philip K. Dick, the author of the original 1968 novel *Do Androids Dream of Electric Sheep?*, on which *Blade Runner* was based, was also a cat lover.)

The term *film noir* was initially used by pre–WWII French film critics, who critiqued the films *The Port of Shadows* (*Le Quai des brumes,* 1938) and *La Bête humaine* (1938) for their moral failings. Film historian Charles O'Brien points out that the term *film noir* first appeared in French journalism as early as 1938 or 1939 as a term of contempt. According to O'Brien, the term originally suggested "an essentially affective response to a group of films that seemed to transgress the morality of the national culture" (O'Brien 1996, 8). In 1939, Georges Altman, a film critic at *La Lumière,* noted about film noir: "THE PUBLIC is embarrassed. The 'critics' are outraged in a fit of morality. Everyone who thinks the cinema is just a dubious form of entertainment or an abject form of pleasure simply cannot understand" (Abel 1988, 266–267). Film historian Nakamura Hideyuki points out that critics used the term *film noir* appreciatively to evaluate the same films as "poetic realism" and/or "avant-garde" that could shock and confuse the viewers for artistic purposes (Nakamura 2009, 78). Thus film noir emerged as a discursive term to assess certain types of films from the perspectives of morality or art.

Then, after WWII, the term *film noir* was applied by French film critics to describe a certain type of Hollywood film—for example, *The Maltese Falcon* (1941), *Double Indemnity* (1944), *Laura* (1944), *Murder, My Sweet* (1944), and *The Woman in the Window* (1944). What the French critics recognized and highly valued was the same quality of "poetic realism" and/or "avant-garde" that they appreciated in some prewar French films and hoped postwar French films could achieve in order to defend the French film industry from the Hollywood invasion (Nakamura 2009, 71). Thus, film noir was never a rigid or pure genre. It appeared in postwar France as a discursive term—like auteurism—and the categorization has since been used in a fluid manner.

### *Shozo, a Cat and Two Women* as a Ghost Cat Film

I propose to consider *Shozo, a Cat and Two Women* as the historical product of genre fluidity. To be specific, despite its apparent status as a successful literary adaptation, I regard this film as an expansion of the ghost cat genre (*kaibyō eiga,* or *bake-neko mono*). The year 1956, when *Shozo, a Cat and Two Women* was released, marked the midst of a boom in ghost cat films. A typical plot of a ghost cat film goes like this: A samurai is killed by his despotic lord, causing the end of the familial lineage. The samurai's wife commits suicide after she begs her cat to avenge the family. The cat that licks the blood of the samurai's dead wife turns into a ghost cat that can freely possess any woman. At the climax of ghost cat films, women possessed by ghost cats always display monstrous actions. They usually jump repeatedly from the tops of castle roofs to the ground and back, and fight against samurai. The stop-trick editing that early filmmaker Georges Méliès often used in his films was adopted. In this style of editing, filming is paused, an object (or a person) is added to or removed from the frame, and the filming restarts. This creates an abrupt teleportation of the monster from one place to another, as in *Black Cat Mansion* (*Bōrei kaibyō yashiki,* Nakagawa Nobuo, 1958). All the samurai can do is be astonished at their agility.

One scene at the seashore in *Shozo, a Cat and Two Women* looks like a ghost cat film scene. Under the bright sunlight, Shinako asks Shōzō to hand over Lily as a remembrance of her life with him. Shinako is in a kimono and crouches on an embankment, showing her back to Shōzō, who stands several feet away. In the close-up of her face that follows, Shinako opens her eyes wide, even though the strong sunlight from above leaves nearly half of her face in shadow. Contrary to her rather scary facial expression, she speaks to Shōzō in a silky voice like a cat's meow: "I can't say I want to come back. But I feel lonely. So give me Lily instead. Please understand a woman's feeling." Then, suddenly, she jumps off the embankment, waving the sleeves of her kimono. Is Shinako jumping into the ocean? Shōzō is as astonished as the samurai in ghost cat films.

In the following shot, Shinako, cat-like, manages to land safely on a rock right under a sign that says "Danger!" Of course, the sign warns that the area is dangerous because of rocks and waves. But to Shōzō, Shinako is the force of danger, asking him to hand over Lily, the cat he loves. In addition, Shinako looks as if such a dangerous action were nothing to her. Then, in a high-angle shot, Shinako comes closer and closer to Shōzō, who runs away in fear to his bicycle, which is parked nearby. Shinako runs after him at full speed. How can she run so fast in her kimono, we wonder? We see that a white handkerchief that she drops clings to the tire of his bike as if it were a segment of a white dress, the typical costume of a Japanese ghost. Shinako's high-pitched, meowing voice calls to Shōzō reproachfully and pursues him as he desperately turns the pedals of his bike. Shinako's monstrous actions—the jump, and the chase in a kimono—look like those of a woman possessed by a ghost cat.

## Shozo, a Cat and Two Women as a Star Film

In addition to the historical context of ghost cat films in Japan, I also want to emphasize the role of the film's two female stars, Yamada Isuzu, who plays Shinako, and Kagawa Kyōko, who plays Fukuko. As we have seen in the previous chapter, auteurism considers filmmaking to be a collaborative effort. An actor, or star, like Marlene Dietrich could play a significant role in creating films about performance and masquerade in 1930s Hollywood, for instance. Here, I argue that the star images of Yamada and Kagawa in this film embodied the changing representations of the female body in the visual culture of postwar Japan.

The kind of socio-historical reading of the star image that I propose has its roots in the recent development of film star studies, which has come to consider the star to be a construction, the result of mediation between producers and audiences/fans within the larger sociocultural dynamic, which includes issues of gender and sexuality, politics, economy, race and ethnicity, age, class, and fashion. Founded on the semiotic and philosophical works on celebrity culture by French philosophers Roland Barthes and Edgar Morin in the early 1970s, film scholar Richard Dyer published his influential book in star studies, *Stars,* in 1979. Dyer argues that a star goes beyond being a real person and becomes an image that is constructed by their performances in films, fan magazine articles, advertising posters, personal biographies, and rumors, among other things, to be consumed as a commodity and/or to represent certain ideologies. Dyer defines a star as a "structured polysemy" and explains the term as "the finite multiplicity of meanings and affects they [stars] embody and the attempt to structure them so that some meanings and affects are foregrounded and others masked or displaced" (Dyer 1979, 30). Dyer believes that a star, as a "real" individual "existence" in the world, succeeds in reconciling the contradictions through "magical synthesis" (Dyer 1979, 95).

As a "real" individual, it was a challenge for Yamada Isuzu, who was the most popular and loved star in late 1930s-1940s Japanese cinema, to play the role of Shinako, an unlovable and monstrous character. Yet by 1956, Yamada was at a difficult stage of her life and her career, undergoing a midlife crisis as she moved into her forties and made the transition from a young and beautiful star to a character actress. The star images of Yamada and Kagawa in this film embodied the changing discourse on female bodies that was valorized in the visual culture of post-WWII Japan. The film is structured so that the historical significance of this changing discourse becomes visible in an (over)emphasized manner, a clear example of Dyer's "magical synthesis."

## Two Ghost Cat Battles

It is noteworthy that *Shozo, a Cat and Two Women* adds scenes that are not in Tanizaki's novel: two battles between Shinako and Fukuko. These two fierce battle scenes must have reminded the audience in 1956 of ghost cat films, both technically and thematically.

The first battle occurs at Shōzō's kitchenware store. Shōzō has gone fishing with Lily. Shinako visits the store, which is empty, and sneaks into it without a sound. The camera enters the dimly lit interior from the bright exterior and goes deeper and deeper into the private space of Shōzō's house behind the store. This is the only clear-cut POV shot used in this film. Shinako invades her enemy's territory, which used to be her own. She calls, "Lily, Lily," in a low voice. If she kidnaps Shōzō's beloved cat, he will definitely beg her to come back. That is her plan. The handheld camera swings a little: the camera operator most likely could not move smoothly with the heavy weight of the 35mm camera on his shoulder. But the sway suitably expresses Shinako's nervous feeling. Curiously, this scene of invasion replicates a scene in *Black Cat Mansion*, in which a female servant visits a room that she thinks is empty. She opens a sliding door without a sound. In a POV shot from the position of the nervous female servant, the camera captures two contrastively lit spaces in a composition with depth: a dimly lit corridor with a black sliding door and a brightly lit room where an elderly woman possessed by a ghost cat licks a wound.

The psychological dynamics of the scene change when Fukuko comes back to the store on her bike. Close-ups of Fukuko's face wearing sunglasses and of Shinako's face backlit by the light coming from the back door appear one after another as shot reverse shots. Because of the sunglasses and the backlight, we cannot see their facial expressions clearly. Suddenly, Shinako, who is in the dimly lit interior, starts laughing with a terrifying hissing sound. It is as if Fukuko has taken over the position of the female servant and Shinako the elderly woman in *Black Cat Mansion*. Trying to keep calm, Fukuko sits at a table, opens the cap on a bottle of milk, and sips some milk, like a cat.

The technique of deep focus, a special cinematographic and compositional technique in which all parts within a frame, from the front to the back, are in focus, is conspicuously adopted here. Orson Welles' *Citizen Kane* (1941) is famous for its extensive use of deep focus. In this scene, Fukuko drinks milk in the forefront, while Shinako remains in shadow at the back of the same shot. Shinako makes a sarcastic remark from the dark: "I sent you three letters. Of course, you read them, didn't you?" In the shot that follows, Shinako's face is placed right in front of the camera. She laughs again with a hissing voice and says, "There is something that I want." Fukuko, recoiling in fear, is at the back in the same shot.

Shinako appears to be in a relatively predominant position, even though it is Fukuko who currently lives in Shōzō's house. Lighting causes this sense of changing hierarchy. Whether Shinako is at the back or in the front of the space, only half of her face is backlit and shines ominously. The lighting, which emphasizes the contrast between light and shadow, especially on Shinako's face, enhances Fukuko's fear and anxiety. In contrast, no conspicuous lighting is used for Fukuko. Agitated, Fukuko cries out hysterically, "Go home, go home! This is my house!" and chases Shinako away.

Depth of field is often used in ghost cat films, with a signature device of the genre called *nekojarashi* (pronounced "nay-koh-jah-la-she"). According to film historian Shimura Miyoko, *nekojarashi* originated in kabuki and imitates "a cat playing with a mouse" (Shimura 2006, 98). In ghost cat films, humans replace the mouse and are toyed with by ghost cats. In a scene from *Ghost Cat of Otama Pond* (*Kaibyō Otamagaike*, Ishikawa Yoshirō, 1960), a young servant is controlled with the act of *nekojarashi* by an elderly woman possessed by a ghost cat. Depth of field in the composition within the frame is utilized in order to enhance the effect of the *nekojarashi*. The young woman stands at the back and the elderly woman in the front. There are slightly open sliding doors in the middle, which emphasizes the power play between two planes in the composition within the frame. If we bear this in mind, Shinako and Fukuko seemingly try to force the *nekojarashi* against each other in deep space. When Shinako's power is about to surpass Fukuko's, Fukuko invokes her territorial power—"This is my house!"

Round two of the battle between Shinako and Fukuko occurs at the doorway of Shinako's sister's house, where Shinako is staying. The battle centers on Shōzō's visit to Shinako. He wants to see Lily, who has been taken away by Shinako. But Fukuko also shows up. She believes that Shōzō is there to secretly see Shinako. This time, the battle goes beyond words. It is raining cats and dogs outside. In addition to the framing, lighting, and editing, the acting of the two women is over the top. As the tone of the non-diegetic sound (i.e., the source of the sound is not visible or implied in the scene) rises dramatically, the two women draw closer and closer. A close-up of the two faces. A long shot of the two closing in on each other. A close-up of Shinako crouching and looking up, in which her face is lit from both sides. The center of her face is in shadow, but her eyes glitter with excitement. Declaring, "I won't lose," Shinako clenches her teeth. Fukuko responds with a fierce facial expression in the close-up that follows. Then comes an extreme close-up of the two, clenching their teeth. Light comes from the paper screen (*shōji*) window on the wall behind and leaves their faces in relative shade. Rain, sweat, makeup, and lipstick make their faces shine darkly. Their teeth gleam with saliva. The two grapple, punch, and pull each other's hair. They do not look like human beings any longer but rather two animals, or two monster cats. Because of the compiling of extreme close-ups, we feel that we are witnessing this grotesque battle right in front of us, even closer than sitting next to a boxing ring. After several minutes of scuffling, Fukuko falls down in the doorway as if she were dead. Then Shinako, in a torn kimono, sobs and leans back against the door. The camera rises up, swaying, as if it were following the souls of the two women leaving their bodies. As the camera captures the two from above in a high-angle shot, the score echoes dreadfully like that in a horror film.

As such, in the climactic battle in *Shozo, a Cat and Two Women*, the focus is on grotesque female faces and bodies. In this sense, this film aligns more closely with the ghost cat films of the 1950s.

## Two Ghost Cats Battle

Even as the film *Shozo, a Cat and Two Women* was made, another battle, influenced by the popularity of the ghost cat films, was taking place off screen between two different women—Yamada Isuzu and Irie Takako, who was the most popular actress in Japan in the 1930s. While Irie was experiencing a resuscitation of her career with the ghost cat genre in the 1950s, Yamada was also trying to deviate from her image as a beautiful star and resurrect herself as a character actress in the same period. A number of traits connected these two actresses, and Yamada must have been aware of Irie's dramatic comeback.

Irie was the first actress in Japan to establish her own production company, Irie Productions, in 1932. Her performance in *The Water Magician* (*Taki no shiraito,* 1933), a modern drama based on Izumi Kyōka's novel and directed by Mizoguchi Kenji, was received particularly well. She played a selfless heroine who devotes her life to the career of the man she loves. After the dissolution of Irie Productions in 1937, Irie contracted with Tōhō, a new film company. She costarred in *Tojuro's Love* (*Tōjurō no koi,* Yamamoto Kajirō, 1937) with Hasegawa Kazuo, the most popular actor of the time.

After the war ended, Irie did not appear in many other films until *Ghost of Saga Mansion* (*Kaidan Saga yashiki,* Arai Ryōhei, 1953), in which she played a woman possessed by a ghost cat. The comeback of Irie Takako, a superstar of silent films renowned for her beautiful face and her sensual body, ignited the third boom of ghost cat films.

While the ghost cat story already existed in kabuki of the Edo period, the first ghost cat film boom came in the Taishō era (1912–1926) when twenty-six films were made. The focus was on the fight scenes between the heroes and the monsters, enhanced by trick cinematography that depicted the immediate transformation of a human being into a monster cat. The second boom arrived in the late 1930s. Twenty-one ghost cat films had been produced by 1940. Many of them starred Suzuki Sumiko, a "vamp" actress of the period. While the second boom relied on Suzuki's physical strength and her sensuality (Shimura 2001, 43), the 1950s ghost cat films focused more on the grotesque display of Irie's face, which is aging, and her body, which lacks sexuality (Shimura 2006, 100). Irie was suffering from Graves' disease, which caused her eyeballs to protrude.

Irie regained her stardom by appearing in *Ghost of Saga Mansion* and four more ghost cat films in four years. The audience of the 1950s ghost cat films not only found thrills in the transformation of a woman into a monster cat but also enjoyed watching the spectacle of the transformed big star. Irie herself was conscious of the connection between the images of monster cats and those of elderly women, as well as the popularity of ghost cat films in contrast to her own falling stardom. She wrote in her autobiography, "After I started appearing in ghost cat films, the roles that came to me became more and more horrible. No matter how terrible those roles were, I was ready to accept any of them as a falling star. But the sad thing was that when they brought those roles to me everyone at our studio stopped telling me, 'I am sorry for asking you to do this kind of a role.' It is a natural thing to happen in this harsh world, though" (Irie 1957, 226).

Like Irie, Yamada started her career during the silent period. Both were stars known for their beauty. A few years after Irie starred in *The Water Magician,* Yamada played leading characters in two modern dramas, *Osaka Elegy (Naniwa erejī,* 1936) and *Sisters of the Gion (Gion no kyōdai,* 1936), both directed by Mizoguchi Kenji. With those two films, Yamada achieved the status of a top actress. In 1938, when Irie's *Tojuro's Love* was released, Yamada also decided to move to Tōhō and soon thereafter co-starred in Naruse Mikio's *Tsuruhachi Tsurujirō* (1938) with Hasagawa Kazuo. The duo of Yamada and Hasegawa was enthusiastically supported by film fans in Japan during the war. During the seven years between 1938 and 1944, as many as seventeen films starring the two were produced, and most became mega hits.

The rivalry between Yamada and Irie was clearly noticeable, especially after Yamada's move to Tōhō. A critic noted, "The master actress [Irie] is having a difficult time in talking pictures. Her status was in danger when Tōhō welcomed Yamada Isuzu to its studio" (Irie 1957, 159). Irie herself "regretfully" admitted that her star status was threatened by Yamada (Irie 1957, 163). Throughout her autobiography, she constantly mentions Yamada and compares her with herself. For instance, she writes, "I noticed that my star status started to collapse around 1946. I didn't know the reason.

I had been a star for seventeen years by then, but as I grew old, I started to lose something like inspiration and self-confidence. I did not have the acting skills of Ms. Yamada Isuzu" (Irie 1957, 174).

This is ironic, because at the time Irie published her autobiography in 1957, Yamada was also distressed by a fear that she, too, lacked acting skills. In her 1953 autobiography, Yamada wrote about this unease:

> I have fortunately received the Yomiuri International Film Festival Special Actress Award, the Mainichi Concours Best Actress Award, and the Blue Ribbon Actress Award [for her roles in *Storm Clouds over Hakone* (*Hakone fūun roku*, 1952) and *The Moderns* (*Gendai-jin,* 1952)], but to be honest I still don't have a systematic approach to acting even after more than twenty years of experiences as a film actress. I stick to what I have learned based on my experiences of appearing in numerous films, but it is still difficult for me to analyze them and construct something methodological. In fact, like anyone who started acting when I did, I was never trained. I did not feel the need and did not practice at it. (Yamada 2000, 143)

Even though such claims could be regarded as mere modesty, it is true that most of the twenty-eight films that she appeared in between 1954 and 1956 were unsuccessful.

Witnessing the sensational comeback of her long-time rival, Yamada decided to play a cat, which she abhorred doing. In 1936, Yamada had said, "I will do any roles, but please do not make me play a cat" (Yamada 2000, 73). In the ghost cat films in which Irie starred, the focus of attraction was the novelty of a superstar from the past playing a monster. It is understandable that Yamada did not like the idea of appearing in a ghost cat film when she was a nineteen-year-old aspiring actress. But in 1956, Yamada gave up her star image of a beautiful modern girl and accepted that she had become an elderly woman. In contrast to Irie's case, the name of Tanizaki and the ghost cat literary genre worked as a safety valve for Yamada. While *Shozo, a Cat and Two Women* was produced during the ghost cat boom and obviously referenced that genre, it was apparently difficult for anyone to categorize the film as a ghost cat film thanks to the illustrious name of Tanizaki. Even if Yamada's image in it seemed similar to a monster cat, it was viewed as a conscious playing-out of the well-known image of a ghost cat. It was regarded as a respectful self-referential performance of vulgarity by an aging actress.

## Becoming Ghost Cats in Postwar Japan

Beyond Yamada's personal ordeal as an aging star and her rivalry with Irie, there existed yet another significant historical background that made it possible to represent women in *Shozo, a Cat and Two Women* as ghost cats. Female representation in visual culture was changing in postwar Japan when the film was released in 1956. In terms of the feline representation of women in the film, there is an emphasis on the corporeality of women's bodies, which look grotesque. Even when women's faces are displayed in close-ups, the focus is not on their beauty but on their corporeality.

The cinematographer of *Shozo, a Cat and Two Women* was Miura Mitsuo, who photographed both Yamada and Irie in their star vehicles in the 1930s and 1940s. Miura's ultimate goal at that time was to make those female stars' faces as beautiful as possible no matter what artificial techniques he used. During the silent film era, Miura had a contract at Irie Productions and photographed three Irie star vehicles. When Irie Productions was dismantled, he moved to Photo Chemical Laboratory (PCL) and worked on *Tōjuro's Love,* a star vehicle for Irie and Hasegawa Kazuo. Then, he photographed *Female Genealogy* (*Onna keizu,* Makino Masahiro, 1942) and its sequel (*Zoku onna keizu,* Makino Masahiro, 1942), directed by Makino Masahiro and starring Yamada and Hasegawa. In both *Tōjuro's Love* and *Female Genealogy,* Miura captured the facial expressions in close-ups and with special lighting of tragic heroines who sacrificed their lives for the careers of men they loved.

At the climax of *Tōjuro's Love,* Tōjurō (Hasegawa), a young kabuki actor, tells O-Kaji (Irie), a geisha, that he loves her. It is a lie. Tōjurō only thinks about his art. A love affair is merely a tool for him to improve his acting skill. He ruthlessly observes O-Kaji's reaction—her facial expressions and her behaviors. The couple is in a room at night. The room is lit only by a paper lantern (*andon*) in the corner. While strong contrasty lighting is placed on the face of Tōjurō, the close-up of O-Kaji, who is truly in love with Tōjurō, is in soft lighting, which makes her look extremely sensual.

At the climax of *Female Genealogy,* Hayase (Hasegawa), a young chemist, tells O-Tsuta (Yamada), a former geisha who loves him, that he cannot see her any longer. Hayase must follow his mentor's order to focus on his studies. The couple is at Yushima Shrine at night. They are lit only by the moonlight. There is no glamorous close-up of the kind typically used in star vehicles. Instead, the couple is photographed in a long shot of long duration (long take). Hayase is almost in silhouette. Because of the distance between the camera and the couple, and because of the low lighting, the beauty of a close-up of O-Tsuta's face in the following scene at a noodle shop is striking.

O-Tsuta's expression of sadness (she must leave him when she does not want to) is emphasized in brighter and softer lighting. The Hollywood-style three-point lighting, which shows a star's face glamorously, is not adopted, though. Rather, Miura faithfully recreated the lighting of a cheap noodle shop, which uses only an uncovered electric bulb above each table.

At the time he worked on these two films, Miura was publicly insisting that he would pursue documentary-style cinematography in opposition to Hollywood style, in which stars were captured in heavenly beauty. In *Cinematography Reader* (*Eiga satsueigaku dokuhon*, 1940), Miura wrote, "Speaking of methods of lighting, I think it is dangerous to be absorbed in blindly imitating foreign films and bringing glamorous brightness into Japanese rooms . . . The beauty of simple and soft beams of light floating into a Japanese room in the semi-dark evening: this is the light that we find most intimate" (Miura 1940, 241–42). Miura thus emphasized the spatial difference between Hollywood and Japan and insisted on adopting different lighting schemes in order to represent them properly. Miura's idea was most likely based on Tanizaki's *In Praise of Shadows* (*Inei raisan*, 1933–1934). Tanizaki's appreciation of darkness and shadow as the essence of Japanese aesthetics and culture was not exactly based on the actuality of the Japanese landscape and architecture of the time. Curiously, this was the time when Japan led the world in the vogue of neon signs. Tanizaki fully understood the formidable attraction of such modern technology as electric lighting. Simultaneously, he was aware of the material limitations in Japan. Tanizaki's conceptual dilemma was the reality of Japanese cinematographers.

Even when pursuing a documentary style in the name of Japanese aesthetics, however, Miura and other Japanese cinematographers highly valued the works of Lee Garmes, who photographed Josef von Sternberg's films starring Marlene Dietrich. They particularly appreciated Garmes's technique, the so-called north light, which enhances the glamour of the star. While the overall tone was dark, the shadows in Garmes's cinematography were not simply black but showed numerous levels of blackness in gradation. In order to achieve that type of lighting, however, it was essential to use large numbers of lamps and very sensitive film stocks. The shortage of equipment and materials in Japan made meeting this requirement hopeless. The appreciation of shadows and the notion of Japanese aesthetics, therefore, appear to be a desperate measure by cinematographers to overcome such limitations. Torn between their yearning for Hollywood and the reality of their situation, Miura and others emphasized the pitch-blackness without the gradations of documentary style.

While Miura publicly insisted on documentary style as the default for Japanese filmmaking, he still wanted to imitate Garmes's artificial glamorous lighting for close-ups of his stars, especially for Irie, Yamada, and Hasegawa. The result was that some criticized his cinematography, saying that the films of Tōhō's studio were "beautiful but without soul" and "lacked Japanese characteristics" (Tsumura 1943, 38–39). The examples of *Tojuro's Love* and *Female Genealogy* were the results of Miura's dilemma and his efforts towards the Hollywood-style artificial beauty of star lighting.

Given Miura's obsession with beauty in close-ups of the stars even during the privations of wartime, how do we respond to the non-glamorous, even grotesque appearance of Yamada in *Shozo, a Cat and Two Women?* When Shinako appears in the film for the first time, she is taking in the washing in a tiny, untidy backyard. She is captured backlit in a medium shot under the strong sunlight. Her face is in the shade. She is looking down, biting her lip, frowning, and wiping the sweat from her face with a worn-out cloth in an irritated manner. After crudely finishing up her work, she rushes upstairs to speak to her mother-in-law. Baring her teeth, she declares that she is leaving: "I cannot stand it any longer." In a medium shot, half of her face is in the shade, but the other half looks greasy and sweaty. It is incredible that the same cinematographer who always tried to photograph the superstar as glamorously as possible now captures the same actress in such a grotesque way. Miura's cinematography in this film adopts more medium and long shots than close-ups in order to capture the corporeal reality of female bodies. Moreover, when close-ups are used, they emphasize such extreme expressions as teeth-baring grimaces and battle-stained faces covered in sweat and saliva. Lighting is not used for glamour but rather enhances the materiality of the body parts. In other words, Miura's cinematography could be understood less as documentary than as connected to representations of bodily excess. Thus, the emphasis of representations shifted from Yamada's face to her body in *Shozo, a Cat and Two Women*. Such a shift of representations corresponded to the changing representations of female bodies valorized in the postwar popular imagination.

During the American occupation that immediately followed Japan's defeat in the Pacific War, one of the reforms was to advance gender equality and ensure women's rights. The idea of women's liberation changed the conventions of gender representation in Japanese cinema under the occupational media policy. Apparently strong-willed, liberated, and independent women emerged on screen in such films as *No Regrets for Our Youth* (*Waga seishun ni kui nashi,* Kurosawa Akira, 1946) and *The Love of Actress Sumako* (*Joyū Sumako no koi,* Mizoguchi Kenji, 1947).

Film scholar Ayako Saito claims, however, "the female body that sustained the new, postwar regime of democracy, at the same time epitomized the contradiction of postwar democratization" (Saito 2014, 331). According to Saito, women's bodies soon became "highly sexualized" in the postwar culture milieu (Saito 2014, 331). Even though Japanese cinema under the occupation did not explicitly show female nudity, the visual presentation of female bodies themselves had a stronger impact than representing them in literary works. While direct visibility of female bodies on screen had a symbolic function towards women's liberation, it also caused objectifying effects on those bodies, especially when they were sexualized. In other words, female bodies were at the same time liberated and objectified during the occupation.

*Shozo, a Cat and Two Women* was released in 1956, four years after the postwar occupation ended, when a new body culture developed in the wake of the Sun Tribe (*Taiyōzoku*) boom and new actors began to emerge. The term *Sun Tribe* came from Ishihara Shintarō's 1955 novel, *Season of the Sun* (*Taiyō no kisetsu*), and was popularized by the weekly entertainment magazines (*shūkanshi*). Ishihara's novel, which won the prestigious Akutagawa Prize in January 1956, depicted the youth culture of the first postwar generation as "cynical, violent, sexually permissive, and suspiciously foreign" (Raine 2001, 202–203). *Season of the Sun* featured wealthy college students who spend their time dancing, drinking in nightclubs, and sailing. What the Sun Tribe boom made clearly visible was a generational clash. Weekly entertainment magazines reported how troubled older audiences were by the youth culture, which seemed to ignore conventional boundaries and disregard Japanese identity. But no matter how immoral the Sun Tribe generation seemed to older audiences, the morality of the older generation was equally questionable. It was seen as tarnished by its subjugation to ultra-nationalism and fascism during wartime, as well as by its instant switch to American-style democracy during the occupation period. In that light, the immorality and cultural hyperbole of the younger generation could be read as criticism of its elders.

This intergenerational conflict was expressed particularly through the portrayal of bodies. The most visible representative of the Sun Tribe was a new star called Ishihara Yujirō, Shintarō's younger brother. As film historian Michael Raine suggests, Yujirō's image when he became a star was clearly connected to his body: "They talked about his 'un-Japanese' strong physique, his long legs, his [Hawaiian-style] *taiyōzoku* clothes, and his [GI style] *Shintarō-gari* hairstyle" (Raine 2001, 211). Critics in 1956 even thought that Yujirō was "too big and too ugly to be a star" (Raine 2001, 216). He was famous, or notorious, for his uneven teeth as well. A studio publicist even compared him to a monster (*kaibutsu*).

Such a monstrous representation of the body was not limited to Yujirō. In the film version of *Season of the Sun* (*Taiyō no kisetsu,* Furukawa Takumi, 1956), for example, female bodies in bathing suits fill the screen in low-level, low-angle shots. Beyond the dichotomy between liberation and sexualization, what is emphasized in these shots are representations of bodily excess. They are commodified bodies in an Americanized manner, as seen on nightclub floors or on the stage of "Miss" contests, but these hyperbolic shots parody and mock the notions of liberation and sexualization themselves.

In *Shozo, a Cat and Two Women,* female bodies are displayed in a manner that goes along with the contradictory discourse on female bodies: liberation and sexualization. In contrast to the representation of Shōzō as a degraded and feminized man, which could be argued to be the iconic image of defeated Japan, the feline representations of Fukuko and Shinako are erotic, athletic, and triumphant. The body of Fukuko is young and sexualized, while that of Shinako is aging but energetic. They are sexually liberated and passionately engaging in resistance to the patriarchal system. Yet, as was the case for the first ghost cat actress, Suzuki Sumiko, naked skin under disordered kimonos made both Fukuko and Shinako erotic objects for the male gaze.

At the same time, the grotesque and monstrous display of female bodies in this film should be located within the intertext of the Sun Tribe boom. In particular, the battle between Shinako and Fukuko could be read as the intergenerational conflict in the form of female bodies. Shinako, played by the biggest star during wartime, represents the morals of the older generation. She is the one who tries to restore the marital order that has been disturbed by conspirators. Fukuko is played by Kagawa Kyōko, who made her debut after the war. In this film, Kagawa clearly plays the new image of the delinquent girl, drinking and dancing at nightclubs and spending her days at the beach with a married man, that was being reported in the popular press and weekly journals around 1956. Since her hyperbolic performance goes against the graceful image that she had presented in such films as *The Crucified Lovers* (*Chikamatsu monogatari,* Mizoguchi Kenji, 1954), a sense of parody comes into her depiction of the Sun Tribe generation.

What characterizes the physical battle scene between Shinako and Fukuko is the sarcastic viewpoint towards the clash between the aging body and the hyper-sexualized young body. As in many ghost cat films of the 1950s, in which an elderly woman who is possessed by a ghost cat torments a young resistant female servant with the technique of *nekojarashi,* Shinako and Fukuko battle over how to take control of their bodies. But the final shot of the battle scene, which is from the ceiling, is illustrative. Both Shinako and Fukuko eventually fall down on the ground in vain, expressing the irreconcilable but not clearly delineated positions between the old and the new in post-occupational Japan. This is ironic, because Yamada herself had played a delinquent girl in *Osaka Elegy* exactly twenty years earlier and had embodied then the anxieties towards the new generation in 1930s Japan.

# CHAPTER 6

# Drawing Pictures of Cats

## National Cinema and Anime in *Jungle Emperor Leo*

*Takeuchi Yoshio, Japan, 1997*

### The Lion King Controversy

When Disney's animated musical film *The Lion King* (Roger Allers and Rob
Minkoff, 1994) was released, the *San Francisco Chronicle* reported "a roar of
protest from those who say the record-breaking animation feature is not as
original as Disney claims but borrows substantially from a Japanese story created 40 years ago." The "Japanese story" was *Jungle Emperor* ( *Janguru taitei*),
a manga by Tezuka Osamu (1928–1989) originally published between 1950
and 1966; an animated TV series (1965–1966) based on the manga was also
broadcast in the United States with the title *Kimba, the White Lion* (1966).
The *San Francisco Chronicle* report listed "similarities" between the two
works: "Both Disney and Mr. Tezuka's animations center on lions in Africa";
"In both, a father lion is the king and is killed early, leaving a young son. The
son returns after an exile and struggles with himself over his responsibility
to become king"; "The son overthrows an evil lion who has usurped the
throne"; and "The good lions are aided by a wise old baboon and a talkative
bird, while the evil lions are aided by henchmen hyenas." The protest against
*The Lion King* was heightened because Disney did not credit Tezuka despite
such similarities.

Curiously, the response from Tezuka Productions in Tokyo was not
critical of Disney. Matsutani Takayuki, president of Tezuka Productions, said,
according to the report, "If Disney took hints from 'The Jungle Emperor,'
our founder the late Osamu Tezuka, would be very pleased by it . . . Rather
than filing a claim, we would be very happy to know that Disney people saw
Tezuka's work. On the whole, we think 'Lion King' is absolutely different
from 'Jungle Emperor' and is Disney's original work."

It is certainly possible to read Matsutani's remarks in the context of a colonial subject pleased to be acknowledged by the more advanced colonial power. Tezuka was a big fan of Disney animation. It is said that he watched *Bambi* (David Hand et al., 1942) eighty times and *Snow White and Seven Dwarfs* (David Hand et al., 1938) fifty times in theaters when these films were released in Japan after World War II ended. He even published manga versions of *Bambi* and *Pinocchio* in Japan in 1951 and 1952 respectively.

Matsutani's statement, which fully respects Disney, can also be located in the history of animation in Japan, and particularly in the context of how Japanese animators adored Disney animations and tried to imitate their styles for a long time. The most common technique of animation has been cel animation, in which pictures are drawn directly onto celluloid "cels." Cel animation began in the United States in 1913. Walt Disney's productions quickly became the benchmark for quality in cel animation. The first talkie animated film, *Steamboat Willie* (Walt Disney and Ub Iwerks), was shown in Japan in 1928. Japanese animators strove to emulate Walt Disney, but they did not know that such productions demanded the resources of a big studio, with large collaborative groups. In Japan, animation was basically a household industry. Typically, a small house was subdivided into smaller rooms for drawing, photographing, and screening, with the bathroom reserved for development. Photography had to be done during daylight hours, between nine and three, to make use of the available light. The camera was set close to the window and operated manually. Family members and relatives constituted the regular staff.

It was only in wartime that animation in Japan received sufficient funding and found its market. Ironically, freed of financial constraints, animators were able to imitate Disney films, the animation style of the enemy. Seo Mitsuyo was the first animator in Japan to work with the multiplane camera, a technique developed some years earlier by Disney to impart a sense of three-dimensional space to animation. In his film *Ants* (*Ari-chan*, 1941), commissioned by the Ministry of Education, Seo could afford to experiment with such costly techniques.

Technical advances and military advances went hand in hand. With the start of the Pacific War in December 1941, the production of animation for propaganda purposes increased. Committed to total war, the Japanese army and government continued to rely on the power of animation to influence audiences. The Ministry of the Navy asked Seo to produce a film to publicize the successful attack on Pearl Harbor. The result was Japan's first feature-length animated film using Disney-style animation, *Peachboy's Sea-eagle* (*Momotarō no umiwashi*, 1943), which ran thirty-seven minutes. In the film, Momotarō, a folklore hero, serves as captain of an aircraft carrier, and various animals (dogs, monkeys, pheasants) pilot his planes. The planes attack Onigashima (the island of Oahu) without sustaining any losses. The film met with resounding success, earning some 650,000 yen (Yamaguchi and Watanabe 1977, 40). One film magazine rated it the third-best film of the year, and there were reports of the Emperor Hirohito's satisfaction when he viewed it. In sum, the wartime government laid the basis for the postwar development of animation, encouraging technical experimentation, training animators, and creating the conditions for teams of animators in the Disney style.

Ōkawa Hiroshi, the first president of Tōei Studios, established Tōei Dōga, the first large-scale animation studio in Japan. At that time, Tōei Studios wished to attract new, larger audiences and thus branched out beyond their characteristic period dramas. Ōkawa hired over one hundred young animators (significantly, only two had received training in wartime animation studios). The air-conditioned ferroconcrete structure itself cost some hundred million yen and was fully equipped with multiplane cameras and other devices developed at Disney Studios (particularly around the production of *Snow White and the Seven Dwarfs*), for Ōkawa Hiroshi aspired to become nothing less than the Walt Disney of the East. Ōkawa's first large-scale work, *The Tale of the White Serpent* (*Hakujaden,* Yabushita Taiji and Ōkawa Hiroshi, 1956), deployed a technique based on live action. It is a technique still used today at Disney Studios in order to create realistic gestures and facial expressions. First, actors are filmed, and after the film is developed, it is transformed into stills that are used to draw the pictures for the animated film. *The Tale of the White Serpent* went on to achieve international success, domestically and internationally. The film was exported to the United States, Brazil, and Taiwan. Not only did it earn 95,000 US dollars, but it also received a prize at the Venice Film Festival. Financially and technically, with *The Tale of the White Serpent,* Tōei Dōga achieved a level of success equal to Disney, at least in the domestic market. As a consequence, many commentators see *The Tale of the White Serpent* as the start of commercial Japanese animation and thus of anime. Indeed, the animator most frequently associated with anime, Miyazaki Hayao, began his career at Tōei Dōga.

Matsutani's statement that *The Lion King* is "absolutely different" from *Jungle Emperor* becomes more interesting when we look at *Jungle Emperor Leo* (*Janguru taitei,* 1997), an animated feature that Tezuka Productions released three years after the controversy around *The Lion King.* Tezuka's manga *Jungle Emperor* has been made into animation several times—three TV series (1965, 1966, and 1989), two theatrical versions (1966 and 1997), one TV film (2009), and one direct-to-video version (1991). Curiously, the 1997 version does not begin from the very beginning of the original manga but from the midst of its story, when Lune and Lukio, the babies of Leo the lion and the respected king of the African jungle, are born. This opening follows *The Lion King,* which starts when the king Mufasa's son, Simba, is born. While *The Lion King* is the coming-of-age story of Simba, *Jungle Emperor Leo* turns into the coming-of-age story of Lune because of narrative choices.

## *The Lion King* vs. *Jungle Emperor Leo*: 3-D and 2-D Styles

While the beginnings of the stories are identical, the images that we see on the screen look quite different. When Matsutani stated that *The Lion King* was "absolutely different" from *Jungle Emperor,* he might have been referring to their styles rather than their stories. The openings of *The Lion King* and *Jungle Emperor Leo* indicate "different" ways of drawing and painting pictures of big cats. Such differences stem from different styles of animation that Disney and Tezuka Productions take despite the long history of Disney adoration among Japanese animators.

Cats have appeared in drawings or paintings since the time they first started living alongside human beings about 4,000 years ago in ancient Egypt. Since Egyptian religious belief viewed all kinds of animals as manifestations of deities, cats too were often depicted as divine beings. Cats are ignored in the Bible, but because of their association with pagan practices, they are treated ambivalently in Christian art, either as a benign presence or a negative symbol of evil. By the seventeenth and eighteenth centuries, cats were often featured in paintings of domestic settings, depicting qualities of femininity, vanity, and playfulness. In the nineteenth century, an increasing number of artists began to portray companionship and affection toward cats, including Édouard Manet and Pierre-Auguste Renoir. These painters were familiar with *ukiyo-e,* Japanese woodblock prints, in which cats were often depicted with natural grace and sinuous contours.

To me, one of the most notable characteristics of cats in drawings and paintings over the years is their speed or quickness. Art historian Caroline Bugler writes, "It is no surprise that some of the most accurate and sensitive portrayals of cats—those that come closest to penetrating their essential nature—are informal pencil or watercolour studies not destined for the public gaze. In these sketches, quickly jotted down on paper, the cat is not part of a painting burdened with allegorical, religious or mythological meaning, or shown as the plaything of women and children in a cozy interior. Shorn of context and free from surroundings, its true character is allowed to emerge" (Bugler 1981, 158). A sketch of a cat appeared as early as c. 1297–1185 BC in

Egypt on smooth white limestone. Since then, such acclaimed artists as Jan Breughel the Elder, Leonardo da Vinci, Paul Gauguin, Manet, and Katsushika Hokusai of Japan left a number of sketches of cats, capturing spontaneous moments and movements. Even in complete paintings, cats often display the essence of sketch—quickness in speed with particular emphasis on touches and brush strokes. For instance, in Renoir's *A Boy with a Cat* (*Le garçon au chat*, 1868), the cat "is tenderly portrayed in broad fluid strokes of paint, which present a contrast with the rather dry treatment of the boy's figure" (Bugler 1981, 146).

*Jungle Emperor Leo* and *The Lion King* adopt different styles in their portrayal of cats and the landscape surrounding them. First of all, in *The Lion King*, the movements of the characters (animals, including lions, in this case) are smooth and flawless. This is a typical example of so-called "full animation." Animation artists take on the task of the movie camera's shutter, drawing a figure in various stages of motion, at relatively equal intervals (LaMarre 2002, 331). They replicate the camera's way of decomposing "live action," but with sketches rather than snapshots. The Disney standard of full animation demanded that the artist draw approximately twelve frames per second. It is common to film live-action sequences in order to produce a series of images to be redrawn by animation artists. This was the practice that Japanese animators at Tōei Dōga tried to imitate when they made *The Tale of the White Serpent*.

Second, the major focus of the opening of *The Lion King* is the emphasis on depth. After the first extreme long shot of the daybreak, there are a series of medium shots of animals (a rhino, horned deer, meerkats, a cheetah, and pelicans). Following a medium shot of a pelican starting to fly, there are a series of extreme long shots. These extreme long shots are typical examples of the multiplane camera, which preceded 3-D computer-generated animation and simulates the visual qualities of three-dimensional space as it is photographed. A flock of pelicans fly in front of giant waterfalls. A herd of elephants walks in the mist in front of a high mountain. A group of flamingos fly over the river as more birds pass across the frame closer to the camera. A herd of horned deer jumps across the frame at back and in front. A baby giraffe appears from behind a hill, accompanied by its mother, approaches the camera, makes a slight left turn, and looks over the hill. What we, the viewers, see with the baby giraffe, which stays in the left front corner of the frame, is a number of different animals walking in the vast field at a great distance. In the same shot, the two giraffes start to run and join the other animals at the far back. In the next shot, a line of bugs carries green leaves on a tree branch in front while a herd of zebras run on the ground behind

Opening of *The Lion King.*

Emphasis on depth.

the tree. A shot of blue birds and elephants running towards the camera follows. Eventually, all these animals gather under a gigantic rock. Following the movement of a flying bird, the camera swiftly approaches the rock where Mufasa stands.

What is important in this scene is photographic realism within the computer-generated illusion of reality. Visual verisimilitude is maintained clearly by linear perspective, which has been an influential approach to realism in Europe since the Renaissance era. Japanese Studies scholar Thomas Looser argues,

> In classic Western perspectival space, everything is unified
> and hierarchized by the single vanishing point; space itself is
> accordingly homogenous, and everything finds its proper place
> within that space, including the spectator (drawn into the picture

plane via the vanishing point), in accordance with fixed mathematical laws of relation. This yields stable positions of near versus far, subject versus object, and, supposedly, the position and identity of the viewing subject. Again, in a depth model, that now seems almost three-dimensional (but qualitatively homogenous). (Looser 2006, 97)

In contrast to the opening of *The Lion King,* that of *Jungle Emperor Leo* does not look fully three-dimensional. First, while nearly all the movements of animals in the opening scene of *The Lion King* were flawless and smooth, we the viewers cannot help noticing Leo's movements with "skippiness, jerkiness, awkwardness" (LaMarre 2002, 338), or the gap between stillness and movement in his actions in the opening scene of *Jungle Emperor Leo.* After a very brief close-up of the moving legs of a white lion, we see Leo running in a dimly-lit grass field in a long shot. Here, Leo's body is not depicted in a realistic manner at all. The shape of his body is drawn only by simple lines, as if it were a caricature. Moreover, while Leo moves his four legs, his tail, and his mane, he does not seem to be running appropriately. The movement of his body parts is too consistent. His body does not move from the center of the frame. Only the grass around him moves from left to right. The situation is similar in the following close-up. Now we see Leo's upper body from the side. It constantly moves, but it seems to be shaking from left to right and not running, especially because the movement of the blue sky at the back is too slight. The shot that follows captures Leo from the front. We see a constant movement of his two front legs only. Gradually, the camera draws back and we start to see Leo's face, but no movement is added to his face at all. This is a typical example of "limited animation," which uses fewer drawings. The result is that we understand that Leo is on the move. We know the big cat is running, but at the same time, we clearly notice that his movements are not realistic in a photographic sense.

In addition to the sense of jerkiness, Leo's movements look very flat. Many of his movements are horizontal or vertical, but not between the front and the back. Leo's approach to his home, a ruin, is depicted as a POV shot, and we do not see Leo physically come close to the place. In cel animation, which uses meticulously painted outline drawings on thin, transparent sheets of celluloid, images are logically displayed in two-dimensional space. Leo himself appears rather flatly drawn because of black-ink character outlines.

It is true that *Jungle Emperor Leo* also uses deep composition. But when cel animation integrates depth, it tends to be represented between layers of composited images. Leo's movements occur in front of the background,

Opening of *Jungle Emperor Leo*.

Leo's movements with "skippiness, jerkiness, awkwardness," even though it is difficult to notice them in still images.

including the waterfall and the sky, which is drawn in multiple layers. When he jumps from the top of a waterfall to the bottom, Leo becomes small then big then small again in an attempt to follow the rules of linear perspective, yet the sizes of the clouds in the sky and the waterfall in the background do not change proportionally. This makes Leo's potentially three-dimensional movement look awkward.

With 3-D computer-generated spaces, when the point of view changes, proportions of objects change accordingly. In contrast, in cel animation, because all the images are drawn and painted by hand, it is difficult to recreate such proportional changes of objects. As a result, when we, the viewers, watch characters movements between front and back, we cannot help noticing the multiple layers in which the images are drawn. Such use of layers is clear in the opening scene when Lune and Lukio watch the movement of a deer, a close friend of Leo, in their POV shot. The deer moves from right to left in front of a number of different animals, but the animals do not move at all. There are two planes in this shot. The animals are painted as flatly as the background in the second plane, and the deer moves in the foreground. This makes his movement look unnatural. Then, in the following shot, an elephant and a giraffe raise Lune and Lukio high in the air using their long trunk and long neck, respectively. The same technique is used: all the other animals on the ground are shown in a flat and static drawing in the background layer. Only Lune, Lukio, the elephant, and the giraffe move in the front layer. Even though the sizes of Lune and Lukio change as they are lifted from the ground, the sizes of the other animals stay the same and do not change proportionally.

Lune and Lukio in the first layer and the other animals in the second layer.

The animals in the second layer are completely static, and their sizes do not change at all.

This creates a strange mismatch in the supposedly three-dimensional movement. In contrast to the photographically realistic image of the African landscape and the drawn-from-live-action movements of animals in *The Lion King,* the landscape in *Jungle Emperor Leo* looks flat and the movements of Leo appear strangely exaggerated.

## "Cool Japan"?: National Cinema and Anime

> Society, customs, art, culture: all are extremely two-dimensional.
> It is particularly apparent in the arts that this sensibility has been
> flowing steadily beneath the surface of Japanese history . . . This
> book hopes to reconsider "super flatness," the sensibility that has
> contributed to and continues to contribute to the construction
> of Japanese culture, as a worldview, and show that it is an original
> concept that links the past with the present and the future. During
> the modern period, as Japan has been Westernized, how has this
> "super flat" sensibility metamorphosed? . . . "Super flatness" is
> an original concept of Japanese who have been completely
> Westernized. (Murakami 2000, 5)

In April 2000, the Japanese visual artist Murakami Takashi curated an exhibition titled *Superflat.* By "super flatness," Murakami refers to various flattened forms in Japanese fine arts and pop culture, including anime. In "The Super Flat Manifesto," the introductory essay to the exhibition catalog, Murakami tries to create a direct lineage between art from Japan's premodern period and contemporary art, including anime and manga. As a first example of superflat, the catalog juxtaposes a series of stills of the explosion of a planet from *Galaxy Express 999* (*Ginga tetsudō 999,* Rintarō, 1979) with a famous woodblock print from Hokusai's *Thirty-Six Views of Mt. Fuji* (*Fugaku sanjūrokkei,* c. 1831). As film theorist Thomas LaMarre describes, "Both images flatten the relationship between different planes (foreground, background, and middle grounds), with zigzagging, arching, sweeping lines that encourage the eye to wander over the surface of the image, restlessly scanning it" (LaMarre 2009, 112). As LaMarre points out, Murakami makes the connection "entirely in terms of the structural composition of the image," which apparently lacks depth (LaMarre 2009, 112). By doing so, Murakami's "superflat" avoids looking at the history of modernization in Japan, which has had a complicated relation to Western technology.

Similarly, Takahata Isao, a noted animator, producer, and director, claims in his 1999 book *Animation in the Twelfth Century: The Cinematic and Animetic in National Treasure Scroll Paintings* (*Jūni seiki no animēshon: Kokuhō emakimono ni miru eiga-teki anime-teki narumono*) that, technically speaking, we should look for the origins of contemporary anime in twelfth-century illustrated hand scrolls or sketchbooks, such as *The Picture Book of Ban Dainagon* (*Ban dainagon ekotoba*) and *Animal-Person Caricatures* (*Chōjū-jinbutsu-giga*). (One cat appears in *Animal-Person Caricatures*. Compared to other animals, the eyes of the cat are drawn nice and big.) By referring to *giga*, Takahata tries to locate the origins of manga and anime in twelfth-century art.

Tezuka adopted the drawing technique of limited animation in his *Tetsuwan Atomu*, Japan's first weekly thirty-minute-long television animation, which started in 1963 and would also become popular in the United States as *Astro Boy*. With its emphasis on exaggerations and omissions, limited animation often results in flat-looking characters and jerky movements, which is entirely different from the drawn-from-live-action animation of Disney.

However, contrary to Murakami's theory of superflat and Takahata's idea of twelfth-century-animation, it is not my intention here to insinuate that the "absolute" difference between *Jungle Emperor Leo* and *The Lion King*, or between limited animation and full animation, might be based on a sense of cultural essentialism that uniquely distinguishes the flat aesthetics of Japan from the depth aesthetics of the West. I do not mean to define anime as a uniquely Japanese art form. I suggest, rather, that it is necessary to have a more historically specific perspective when we discuss the connections and differences between Disney animation, anime, manga, and *giga*.

For instance, woodblock prints by Hokusai flatten the hierarchal relationship of depth between the front and the back of a surface, as Murakami insists in "The Super Flat Manifesto." However, historically speaking, many of the Edo artists knew and understood Western geometric perspective perfectly and used it "as one among many modes of spatial organization that could be played with, and even layered over other kinds of space" (Looser 2006, 101). Some of Hokusai's images play with two or more viewpoints within the same image, inviting the viewers not so much to reject depth as to layer viewpoints. Moreover, as we have already seen, the history of anime in Japan has been full of admiration and understanding of the full animation of Disney. These historical periods, when Hokusai worked and when anime developed, certainly existed between the flatness of *giga* and the apparently flat-looking limited anime.

My suggestion about historical awareness is a response to "Cool Japan," a concept coined in 2002 by journalist Douglas McGray and later adopted by the Japanese government. "Cool Japan" expresses Japan's growing cultural superpower and the extremely competitive products of a global capitalist economy. In the Japanese government's "Cool Japan" campaign, as Prime Minister Abe Shinzō's appearance in disguise as Super Mario at the closing ceremony of the 2016 Olympic Games in Rio de Janeiro demonstrated, anime has been regarded as uniquely representative of Japanese culture, despite its complicated historical relationship with Disney.

The choice of anime and its emphasis on superflatness without historical specificity in the "Cool Japan" discourse reminds us of the post-WWII attempt of the Japanese film industry to formulate a "national cinema" that would represent Japan's unique culture. In film studies, studies of "national cinema" since the late 1970s have emphasized that cinema has the function of realizing a nation. Film theorist Stephen Heath argues that nationhood is not given but is rather something to be "gained," and that cinema is one of the means by which it is "gained" (Heath 1978, 10). Film scholars Ella Shohat and Robert Stam also suggest the role of cinema in the process of imaginary construction of national identity (Shohat and Stam 1996, 153–154). Clearly, Shohat and Stam follow historian Benedict Anderson and his idea of national self-consciousness as the precondition for nationhood. Anderson argued that collective consciousness about origins, status, location, and aspirations became possible due to the use of common language in the novel and the newspaper, the products of print capitalism (Anderson 1983, 41–46). Similarly, cinema can actively work to construct collective consciousness, rather than simply reflecting or expressing an already fully-formed and homogenous national culture and identity.

By the late 1950s, when *Shozo, a Cat and Two Women,* the film discussed in the previous chapter, was released, Japanese cinema had recovered from the devastation of World War II, largely thanks to the strong support of the Allied Occupation (1945–1952), and was enjoying its golden period. According to the report by the Motion Picture Producers Association of Japan (Nihon eiga seisakusha renmei), in 1958, motion pictures reached an unprecedented 1,127,452,000 viewers. The number of Japanese films released in 1960 rose to an unprecedented 547. The number of film theaters increased to 7,457 in 1960. (In comparison, in 1996, the number of viewers was 119,575,000, about one-tenth that of 1958.) The number of Japanese films released in that year was 278; most of them were independent films, whereas most of the 547 films of 1960 were produced by major film studios. The number of theaters dropped to 1,828 (www.eiren.org/toukei/data.html). Audiences were particularly attracted by genre films such as melodrama, comedy, and horror (monster films).

Simultaneously, a number of Japanese films received critical acclaim in international film festivals in the 1950s. Kurosawa Akira's *Rashomon*

(*Rashōmon*, 1950) received the Golden Lion prize at the Venice International Film Festival in 1951. Mizoguchi Kenji's *Ugetsu* (*Ugetsu monogatari*, 1953) received the Silver Lion prize in 1953 at Venice, and his *Sansho the Bailiff* (*Sanshō dayu*, 1954) was awarded the same prize in 1954 along with Kurosawa's *Seven Samurai* (*Shichinin no samurai*, 1954). Kinugasa Teinosuke's *Gate of Hell* (*Jigokumon*, 1954) followed with the Grand Prize at the 1954 Cannes Film Festival. As a result, the term "Japanese cinema" spread among international critics and audiences for the first time.

This was followed by a conscious and strategic attempt to construct a national cinema. The unexpected success of *Rashomon* at the Venice festival had a certain influence upon Japanese state policy makers and impacted the way Japan would publicize its new image in the post-WWII reconstruction era (Davis 1996, 31–36). Nagata Masaichi, the president of Daiei Studio, which produced the film, became aware of certain expectations from international audiences towards Japanese cinema. He strategically initiated producing and exporting films that paid little attention to the historical accuracy of their contents but emphasized hyperbolic Japaneseness, or traditional-looking cultural objects such as scroll paintings (*emaki*), gorgeous kimonos, sword-fighting samurai, etc. *Gate of Hell* was one such example.

So, two types of films existed in Japan in the 1950s: genre films and exotic films. While the former were well received in Japan, it was the latter that were formulated and recognized as the Japanese national cinema. Nagata's strategy, which mixes and matches traditional cultural elements while paying little attention to historical accuracy and specificity, can be called the self-exoticization of Japanese cinema and culture. The major justification for these films was their appeal to foreign viewers. Thus, the expectations of the international "gaze" at the Japanese culture initiated the formation of a national cinema in Japan. *Gate of Hell* was not very successful in the Japanese market, probably because it was regarded as too exotic. Yet, the self-exoticization policy strategically adopted by the Japanese film industry in the 1950s provided an opportunity for the Japanese spectator to consciously think about what Japanese culture was and would be.

## Impressionism and Its Expression of Movement

The construction of anime as representative of Japanese culture in the current "Cool Japan" campaign is mostly market-dictated. Instead of simply connecting Tezuka and *giga* in the name of superflatness and Cool Japan, I propose that *giga* artists and Tezuka shared a major concern of how to capture movements at different historical moments. Moreover, I suggest that there was a transnational and cross-cultural dialogue on how to capture movements that went beyond the ahistorical, culturally essentialist connection between caricatures and anime in the name of superflatness.

In his book on the *Hokusai Manga* (1814–1878), a collection of *giga* on various subjects by the Japanese artist Katsushika Hokusai (1760–1849), art historian and manga scholar Shimizu Isao argues that for Hokusai the skill of a graphic artist lies in his/her ability to precisely convey movements, such as water and waves and human bodies (Shimizu 2014, 222). For that purpose, Shimizu claims Hokusai included consecutive sketches of human and animal bodies and analyzed their muscle movements.

According to Shimizu, cats appeared more than any other animal in *giga*. Hokusai was particularly fond of big cats on the move. "Running Tiger" ("*Hashiru tora*") in *Hokusai Manga* captures the accelerating movement of a tiger. A shower of blossoms that surrounds it enhances the sense of the moment. Similarly, in "A Lion That Is About to Jump" ("*Tobiagarantosuru shishi*"), the moment is conveyed by concentrating on the lion's muscles, depicted with rough touches of the brush. The positions and shapes of the tiger's legs and claws as well as the lion's rigidly posed body and spinning tail are not photographically real but exaggerated. Still, they clearly look as though they are on the move.

The sketching skill of Japanese artists that was displayed in *Hokusai Manga* drew particular attention in Europe as early as 1856 (Inaga 1997, 276). "The attraction of sketching," according to Maurice Letouzé, who reviewed the Japanese paintings at the 1900 Exhibition in Paris, "comes from precise and graceful techniques that nobody can deny. . . . The best example of how Japanese painters display their masterful techniques with their hands is in their representation of animals. See the two tigers by Ōhashi Suiseki. One of them is resting half of its body and yawns with its mouth wide open. The other tiger, which has just climbed upon a rock, turns around and shows its grin, the grin that characterizes cats" (qtd. in Tano 1990, 445). Théodore Duret, a critic and an advocate of Impressionism, noted, "Japanese artists, who cannot withdraw once they place their brushes on their canvas, stabilize images with their brushes in their raised arms without a break. Their boldness, easiness, and sureness are out of reach for Western artists, who have other capabilities and skills. Because of their tastes, it is worth noting that Japanese people are the first and the most perfect Impressionists" (qtd. in Inaga 2014, 103).

One of the goals of Impressionist painters was to capture a moment in their work. The attempt included a strong awareness of the impossibility of such an act, referred to as *instantaneity*. Instantaneity (*l'instantanéité*) was a word that Claude Monet used to describe his project of capturing the land-scape on site, under the exterior light (Mutobe 2007, 171). Instantaneity is not equal to an instant. No matter how hard a painter may try, it is impossible for him/her to complete a painting in an instant. It takes a certain amount of time, and there are always delays. Impressionist and Postimpressionist paint-ers were conscious of this temporal gap between a particular moment and the time it took to create the painting. They understood that it was impos-sible for any human eyes and hands to extract an instant from time or a moment from moving objects. But they tried to represent with their hands the movement that they sensed with their eyes.

## Tezuka's Limited Animation: A Project of Instantaneity under Financial Restriction

Critic Ōtsuka Eiji claims that Tezuka was not really interested in "moving pictures" in his animation; rather, he was obsessed with making his images "look alive" by capturing movements. Tezuka wrote in 1980, "From the cave drawings of the Primitive Era and through the Renaissance, Baroque, and Modern eras, how hard the painters labored to make their pictures 'look alive.' The word animation derives from anima, a living thing. A living thing moves without fail. It is animation that draws this movement in pictures" (qtd. in Ōtsuka 223). For instance, in Tezuka's manga *Film Is Alive* (*Firumu wa ikiteiru*, 1958–1959), two wannabe-animators, Musashi and Kojirō, com-pete to draw a picture of a flying swallow with their pens as if it were alive. Looking at Musashi's sketch, done quickly in both hands, Kojirō is excited and says, "It looks as if it were alive!" Still, Musashi is told by an elderly manga artist, "Movement is dead in your drawings. Film is alive!" For Tezuka, manga might have been about editing, but animation was about still images that capture movement. Such images do not need to depict objects in a photographic manner.

What is the value of animation if it redraws and repaints photographic images, as Disney does? To me, this was the question that Tezuka asked. Tezuka's attitude towards sketches goes beyond photographic realism and shares concerns with Impressionist painters and their projects of instantane-ity. Even though he was a big fan of Disney animation, his sense of animation was that it involved exaggeration and omission, rather than reproduction of live footage. Such omission included three-dimensionality.

Tezuka's obsession with capturing movements in limited numbers of images with exaggeration and omission could also be regarded as a project of instantaneity. With sketches, the artist's physical presence—the movements of his/her brushes—is also captured in images. Art historian James H. Rubin states, "Before Impressionism, and still at the official academies, such free-form, sketch-like paint handling was discouraged in favor of objective-seeming and smoothly crafted illusions of reality. Evidence of the artist's touch should be suppressed so that the artist's 'presence,' manifest through such physical evidence, would not interfere with convincing realism" (Rubin 2003, 118). In particular, sketches of cats often exemplified such an attitude. For instance, Rubin argues, "Manet often engaged playfully and ironically with forms and conventions. And it is no accident that there is more lively brushwork for the cat [in *Young Woman Reclining, in a Spanish Costume,* 1862, Yale University Art Gallery] than elsewhere in the picture, or that the cat is above the artist's name in the dedication to Nadar. Both the brushwork and the cat on which he used it were like a 'signature'—aspects of Manet's repertory and style as distinctive as his handwriting" (Rubin 2003, 23).

Similarly, the aesthetician Paul Souriau argues that photographic images are, in a sense, physiologically false; they fail to represent movement as we really see it, since what is lacking is the real token of movement—its luminous tracing or visible wake (Souriau 1983, 114–121). Thus, the artistic mode that, for Souriau, is most conducive to the representation of movement is the sketch. It is as if the speed, momentum, and necessary imprecision of the sketch embodied all the attributes of our perception of motion. In other words, in the animation of Tezuka Productions, there was an attempt to reclaim the physicality of human eyes and human hands that were attempting to capture and represent movements instantly. Leo's jerky movements look coded to express his joy and excitement about the birth of his own children in the opening of *Jungle Emperor Leo.*

Contrary to recordings by a motion picture camera, the amount of physical labor required of human beings is much larger in the production of animation. But the result seems to evade issues of subjectivity, agency, and intentionality in the case of Disney productions. Just as a motion picture camera can bring viewers to a world in which no human emotion can be detected, Disney-style animation can ultimately wipe out the traces of human activities from the world.

In contrast, Tezuka's animation is an attempt to reproduce an act of physical, bodily actions that tries to capture movement instantaneously. The maximum exaggeration and omission in limited animation is to have a single static drawing/painting and to make it appear to move. This is also the idea behind Japanese sketches and caricatures. However, it is necessary to note that Tezuka's choice was also a result of the financial conditions that he was under when he started working on *Tetsuwan Atomu* in 1963. In the 1960s, it was said that it would take nearly six months to make a thirty-minute Disney-style animation. Constrained to work with drawings that could be sustained for five or six frames, Tezuka adopted different strategies for conveying movement with full animation. He would often emphasize the most visually and emotionally important poses, which could last over many frames, and suppress intermediate movements. This resulted in jerky actions, or explosive and uncontained transitions. Another strategy was to move the drawing, especially the background, rather than to draw the movements.

While the technologies of animation were developed along with industrialization and mechanization, Tezuka's work displays an intention to maintain or restore the physicality of the artist. Moreover, with the jerky and awkward movements of the characters, Tezuka's animation inevitably created awareness of how movements are created in animation. Like the work of Impressionist painters by way of Japanese caricatures, Tezuka's work challenged the supremacy of photographic realism, the idea based on the long tradition of linear perspective in Western aesthetics, in which the spectator is provided with only a single viewing position. With limited animation, we, the viewers, cannot help noticing the techniques of moving images and, consequently, having more attentive viewing positions. Such attentiveness to the images as well as to the history of anime is what we need when we look at anime, especially when they are publicized under the strong influence of the national campaign of Cool Japan.

# CHAPTER 7

# Moving Like a Cat

## Realism in *Take Care of My Cat*

Jeong Jae-eun, South Korea, 2001

### The Young Girls of Incheon

Writing about *Take Care of My Cat* (*Goyangireul Butakhae*), film critic Hasumi Shigehiko says "The viewers are drawn back to severe reality every moment. All they can do is to simply stare at the insecure behaviors of the young women being hurt by the harsh reality" (Hasumi 2008, 226). The film is surely about the "severe" and "harsh reality" of Incheon, a port city located in northwestern South Korea, about 30 miles from Seoul. All the scenes are photographed on location, either in the big city of Seoul or in the industrial port city of Incheon, which is connected to Seoul with buses and railways; this makes this film more susceptible to contingency, or accidents, in many ways. The film depicts the lives of five twenty-year-old girls who have graduated from the same high school. Tae-hee (Bae Doona) helps in her father's sauna and volunteers by taking dictation from a poet who lives with cerebral palsy. Hae-joo (Lee Yo-won), the center of the group, works at a brokerage firm in Seoul and dreams of becoming a career woman. Bi-ryu (Lee Eun-shil) and Ohn-jo (Lee Eun-jo), twins from a family of Chinese origin, cheerfully work at a street stall. Ji-young (Ok Ji-young) cares for her grandparents, with whom she has grown up, in their dilapidated house while she looks for a job. The five girls have been close friends but face heart-breaking changes and difficulties as they enter the real world.

### Three Types of Cinematic Realism

I should say a few words about "realism" in relation to the history of cinema here. Roughly speaking, there have been three major lines of thoughts on cinematic realism: Bazinian realism, psychological realism, and Brechtian realism.

First, Bazinian realism. In the nineteenth century, before the birth of cinema, there were novelists, including Balzac, Stendhal, Flaubert, and George Elliot, who pursued literary naturalism. They told stories of working-class lives and the phenomenal world in a detailed manner, depicting details such as where people lived, what they ate, and how they spoke. One of their goals was to advocate democracy and equality within society. At the birth of cinema, as film scholar Laura Marcus claims, filmic "realism" was "identified with literary naturalism" (Marcus 2007, 180). Film critic André Bazin further emphasized the welter of details of the phenomenal world that the camera can mechanically reproduce. In the late 1920s to early 1930s, during the transition from silent to talkies, it was believed that cinema could represent the daily lives of people as they were, because of the acquisition of sound. Even though films were still in black and white, this belief was strongly shared by filmmakers in post-WWII European countries. Italian Neorealist films, for example, depicted the reality of devastated cities. Inspired by these films, Bazin insisted that the motion picture camera's capability of mechanical reproduction was at the core of cinema's realism. In his 1945 essay, which was later retitled "The Ontology of the Photographic Image," Bazin argued,

> Originality in photography as distinct from originality in painting lies in the essentially objective character of photography. For the first time, between the originating object and its reproduction there intervenes only the instrumentality of a nonliving agent. For the first time an image of the world is formed automatically, without the creative intervention of man ... All the arts are based on the presence of man, only photography derives an advantage from his absence. (Bazin 1960, 7)

For Bazin, cinema records the space of objects and between objects automatically and impartially. In that regard, he highly valued long takes, for instance, in which one shot lasts for a long duration of time without a cut, and deep focus as the notable techniques of cinematic realism that faithfully represent the reality. In a long take, time flows continuously as in the real world because there is no cut in the middle. In a shot with deep focus, everything visible is in focus. For Bazin, both techniques help a film to appear more realistic. In fact, however, cameras, lighting, and microphones, etc., need to be carefully orchestrated in order to achieve successful long takes and deep focus. In that sense, the images with long takes and deep focus are created so artificially that it is difficult to say they faithfully represent the actuality. In any case, Bazinian realism thus connected a theory about the cinematic medium's material and technological nature (automatism or mechanicality) to its technical devices and stylistic practices (long takes and deep focus).

Second, psychological realism. Bazin claimed that the "personality of the photographers" entered into the production by "automatic means" and was limited only to their "selection of the object to be photographed and by way of the purpose he has in mind" (Bazin 1960, 7). While Bazin did not clearly address what he meant by "the purpose," film scholar Dudley Andrew claims that it was "clear" for Bazin:

> [E]ither a filmmaker utilizes empirical reality for his personal
> ends or else he explores empirical reality for its own sake. In the
> former case the filmmaker is making of empirical reality a series
> of signs which point to or create an aesthetics or rhetorical truth,
> perhaps lofty and noble, perhaps prosaic and debased. In the latter
> case, however, the filmmaker brings us closer to the events filmed
> by seeking the significance of a scene somewhere within the
> unadorned tracings it left on the celluloid. (Andrew 1976, 145)

According to Andrew, the dichotomy can be rephrased as "an opposition between narrative realism and perceptual realism" (Andrew 1976, 163). "If perceptual space and time are rendered with honesty, a narrative will lie obscured within the ambiguities of recalcitrant sense data," explains Andrew, and "If, on the other hand, narrative space and time are the object of a film, perceptual space and time will have to be systematically fragmented and manipulated" (Andrew 1976, 163).

If we follow Andrew's view, then so-called classical Hollywood cinema, the majority of films produced at Hollywood studios from the 1930s to the 1960s, is a typical example of narrative realism. As film scholars David Bordwell, Kristin Thompson, and Janet Steiger argue, the verisimilitude of Hollywood cinema is supported by the specific forms of filmmaking and artificial techniques, including framing, lighting, and continuity editing, which are used so seamlessly that the viewers do not notice. As a result, the stories in those films look as if they are happening in real life, even when the three-point-lighting, for instance, does not usually exist in the real world. With these techniques, Hollywood cinema makes it easy for the viewers to identify with, in many cases, a goal-oriented, good-looking, and idealized protagonist. At the same time, as we discussed in the earlier chapter on feminist film theory, Hollywood cinema often leads the viewers to share the protagonist's voyeuristic viewpoint, while prompting identification with the gaze of the camera. *Psychological realism* is another term to describe this type of cinema. Some critics, especially the Marxist ideological critics of the 1970s, often considered this type of realism to be illusionistic.

Third, Brechtian realism. In opposition to seamless and illusionist realism that reduces the audience to passive spectators, the so-called modernist films, which are directly or indirectly influenced by the ideas of poet and playwright Bertolt Brecht and others, make the audience aware of the artificial techniques of filmmaking. Moreover, in contrast to Bazinian realism, which takes only theoretical (or phenomenological) account of the audience, Brechtian realism requires active involvement from the actual viewers of the films. In the 1930s, Brecht explored modernist alienation effects and theatrical distanciation in his pursuit of realism in theater. He acknowledged the entertainment value of realist literature, yet he thought it was necessary to let the audience realize that those stories were artificial. In order to do that, he made his method and process of storytelling visible to the audience. His actors spoke directly to the audience. By doing so, he let the audience know that they were looking at artificially created performance.

## Realisms in *Take Care of My Cat*

One of the fascinating things of *Take Care of My Cat* is the smoothness or lightness of the moves from one form of cinematic realism to another. As Titi, the stray kitten that Ji-young has found, moves from one girl to another, we witness seamless transitions from one realism to another. In addition to Bazinian realism, this film utilizes classical Hollywood realism. Artificial techniques are used so seamlessly that we notice them only with difficulty. At the same time, the film incorporates Brechtian realism, which lets us know how artificially the story is told. Even when it depicts the harsh reality that Hasumi points out, *Take Care of My Cat* does not lose the sense of lightness, which is reminiscent of a cat walking in the street. That cat-like lightness is part of the beauty of this film.

The opening of the film is a good example of the smooth movement from one type of cinematic realism to another. The first shot shows five high school girls in school uniforms. Apparently, they have just come out of their graduation ceremony. In a composition with deep focus, Tae-hee and the twins are in front in an extreme close-up. When they laugh hysterically and go out of the frame, we see Hae-joo and Ji-young walking arm in arm and

Bazanian realism: Long take of five high-school girls.

intimately speaking to each other. Then, Tae-hee and the twins jump back into the frame. Following their constant movements, the handheld camera sways wildly and catches up with them at the pier of a dock. There is no cut up to this point; it is one long take. Bazin would surely praise this opening shot as an ideal example of realism in cinema. After the first long take, shots change one after another for no specific reason. The five girls sing songs, skip ropes, and make a fuss at the pier. Factory buildings of Incheon are clearly visible behind them. The scene looks full of freedom, lightness, and energy. Under the sunny sky, the lighting is very bright and the images are a little too overexposed. It is like an amateur home movie. Even when Tae-hee tries to take a photo in order to capture the moment, the other girls keep moving around. It is difficult for her to place them within a frame. In this sense, these girls are also as cat-like as Holly, Audrey Hepburn's character, in *Breakfast at Tiffany's*.

Following this prologue, the main story of this film begins. The first shot is long and static, and shows the exterior of an apartment building. It is not fancy. This time, relatively underexposed lighting emphasizes the dark atmosphere. We hear a couple quarreling, and something is thrown that breaks a glass window from inside. There is a staircase right next to the apartment. Through a small open window on a landing, we see Hae-joo in a red leather jacket walking down the stairs. For a moment she even looks framed, captured like a prisoner. Then the camera smoothly follows her coming out of the building and walking down a street where some snow still remains. A crane is used for this shot, which craftily keeps Hae-joo at the center of the frame. A sentimental score quietly begins as the camera moves to follow her. The following shot captures her back as she walks up the stairs of a train station. From the apartment building to the station, the locations have

Hollywood realism: Hae-joo (Lee Yo-won) is framed in a small window.

Hollywood realism: The camera follows Hae-joo.

changed drastically. But because the camera keeps showing Hae-joo's back, we do not really think about the change of shots.

In addition, the words "Way Out" are clearly visible on a sign in front of the station where Hae-joo is headed. The sign seems to express her feeling of being captured and her hope of escaping from her parents, who are always fighting with each other. Camera movements, lighting, editing, music, and props—all these techniques are used so seamlessly that we are not aware of them unless we pay close attention to those techniques. Yet, we think we start to understand Hae-joo's family circumstance and emotional condition as real. This is also how psychological realism works in classical Hollywood cinema.

One of Hae-joo's escape methods is her mobile phone. She thinks that, via her phone, she can communicate with everyone in the world freely

Hollywood realism: . . . to the station.

Brechtian realism: Hae-joo texts to her friends.

without being confined anywhere. As soon as she gets on a commuter train to Seoul from the Incheon station, she takes out her cell phone and starts emailing. In other words, she simultaneously starts her physical, geographical movement and her virtual, electronic movement. Suddenly, on the film screen that we are watching, the screen of her cell phone appears beside the image of Hae-joo, who stands right next to a window of the train. The characters that she types now become visible to us. "I think you are still sleeping. Tomorrow at seven. Club 369. Sent." Here, a virtual space and a real space are visible at the same time. It is impossible in real life for a cellular image to appear next to a human, of course; we all know that. But here, an artificial technique of double exposure or subtitling is presented as such and clearly indicates to the viewers that this is a film and that this is an artificial story. This is Brechtian realism.

Hae-joo arrives at her office earlier than anyone else. She opens the blinds one after another. The room becomes brighter. Right next to Hae-joo's back, we see a glass partition on which a world map is designed with digital dots. We have just seen Hae-joo's cellular screen in almost exactly the same position next to her in the previous shot on the train. It seems to symbolically express that the virtual spaces of digital media are the only world where she feels liberated. The title, *Take Care of My Cat,* appears on the glass.

Thus, within less than three minutes and thirty seconds and even before the title is introduced, this film crosses times between the past and the present. At the same time, it moves across three different types of cinematic realism.

## Reality in *Take Care of My Cat*

In *Take Care of My Cat,* the harsh reality is represented as some kind of prison that the five girls are locked inside. Just as Hae-joo appears to be captured within a small window frame in the opening scene, a number of frames within the motion picture frame confine these girls in little spaces. Such "imprisonments" of the five girls are achieved by similar methods of framing in *Breakfast at Tiffany's,* which are used to depict the "confinement" of Holly.

The composition of a shot in which Ji-young looks out from a small window of her room in the attic is almost exactly the same as the one in the opening scene. Like Hae-joo, Ji-young is tightly framed in the small window. Ji-young goes out onto the roof in search of a kitten, and a part of it suddenly collapses. She is literally stuck in the hole, a prisoner of the dark, dilapidated house. Ji-young is also chained, figuratively, to her old grandparents, who need her constant care. She is confined in a claustrophobic space surrounded by pillars and the handrails of staircases. Dust and sand constantly fall from the broken ceiling, which has been patched up with old newspapers. Her grandfather plays the television and radio at full volume. Her grandmother cannot chew kimchi with her artificial teeth. Irritated, Ji-young picks up a big kitchen knife. She means to use it for the kimchi, but the flash of the knife scares a visitor who happens to enter the house at that moment.

The dilapidated house eventually collapses one day while Ji-young is away, killing her grandparents. Ji-young is placed in a cell at a juvenile training facility. She stops talking there. She locks her voice—and her emotions—inside her body.

Tae-hee, who is forced to help at her father's sauna for free, is also confined in her house. On the living room wall is a thickly framed family photo centering on the despotic father. She needs to lock herself into her room in order to secure a time and space of her own. Even when the family eats out, her father is oppressive enough to decide where everyone sits and order what everyone eats. The variety of dishes on the menu of the American-style BBQ restaurant does not help at all. Completely disgusted, Tae-hee covers her face with her hands and curses, "It is abusive to take away our freedom of choice!"

For Ji-young, who dreams of becoming a designer but cannot find a job, Hae-joo, who works at a first-class brokerage firm in Seoul, is a star. Yet even Hae-joo is clearly told by her female boss, a career woman whom she adores, that it is impossible for her to be promoted without a higher educational background. Frustrated, Hae-joo becomes absorbed in a computer game screen at an amusement park.

Elderly care, patriarchy, and "degree-ocracy." These girls rebel against these harsh realities. Tae-hee tries to liberate her emotions and thoughts through her volunteer work with the disabled poet. On the film screen that we see, Hangul characters appear as she types the poet's reading voice into her electric typewriter. Tae-hee's typewriter offers the same release as Hae-joo's cell phone. That is, the digital screen of her typewriter is her emancipated world. But in the end, she comes to know that all this poet wants is to keep her in this small, dark room forever.

Both Ji-young and Hae-joo try to feel different and free by changing their physical appearances. Ji-young dyes her hair. Hae-joo gives up contact lenses, throws away her unfashionable glasses, and undergoes laser surgery. Ji-young buys the latest, coolest-looking mobile phone, borrowing money from her friend to do so. Hae-joo obsessively spends money on dresses that she does not even wear.

Yet, Ji-young's dyed hair is only laughed at by Hae-joo, whose physical obsession intensifies; now she works on her eyes, nails, nose, and so on and on. Her overconsumption endangers her friendship with the other girls.

The virtual network of mobile phones does not work as a tool that connects them, either. Anthropologist Arjun Appadurai insists on deterritorialized connections between imagined selves and imagined worlds by way of "electronic media" (Appadurai 1996, 4). But among the girls in *Take Care of My Cat,* electronic media only works to frustrate them because it does not connect them at the right moments. Ji-young's phone never rings when she is waiting for Hae-joo at a café for many hours. Ji-young never answers the text messages that she constantly receives from Tae-hee. For whatever reason, it is always Tae-hee who needs to pay a visit and talk with each of them. It is symbolic that the screen we see splits into four when all five girls make a conference call (the twins are in one split frame), discuss their friendship, and try to decide on a place to meet. The technique of a split screen implies

Five girls split, despite being connected by their mobile phones.

that though they seem to be connected, in fact, there are clear boundaries between them. Only when Tae-hee and Ji-young exchange cigarettes and smoke them at the same time and place, after their phone connection fails, do they start to understand each other. In other words, their mobile phones become useful for the first time when they do not work properly.

## Moving like a Cat

Now a cat appears in the film. Ji-young finds a kitten on her way back home from her job search. She names it Titi. Director Jeong Jae-eun says of *Take Care of My Cat,* "I wanted my characters to be girls who possessed nothing permanent and therefore were able to leave. Their relationships change and the girls continue to walk. I believe that if something is not moving, the energy weakens and it needs to be filled with things that are moving" (Shin 2005, 128). The kitten Titi is the one who keeps moving, who hates control, and who cannot be easily confined. As if the director wanted her female protagonists to find a way out of systematicity, she lets them keep walking in the city of Incheon and beyond throughout the film.

No one can confine Titi. The kitten is constantly on the move. Ji-young's grandparents do not like to keep it in their confined space. They tell Ji-young that a stray cat will bring bad luck to the house and force her to get rid of it. Ji-young cannot object because it was her grandparents who raised her in their dilapidated house after her parents died. She leaves Titi with her best friend Hae-joo on her twentieth birthday.

At first, Hae-joo seems happy about receiving a special gift from her best friend. However, the next morning Hae-joo returns Titi to Ji-young, saying simply, "I cannot have her." But it is also difficult for Hae-joo to keep a cat: her life is also tightly structured, at least financially. She is not as free and independent as Ji-young thinks.

When Ji-young loses her house and her grandparents, she leaves Titi with Tae-hee, the only friend whom she can trust. Tae-hee has visited her house several times as well as come to her grandparents' funeral. But it is also difficult for Tae-hee to keep the kitten because her life is fully controlled by her father, so she tries to hide Titi in a suitcase in the garage of her house. Tae-hee is not as free and independent, either, as Ji-young hopes.

Every time the kitten is confined, however, it finds a way out. First, Titi slips out through a window of Ji-young's dilapidated attic. Ji-young chases her and becomes stuck in the hole on the roof, in the scene I discussed earlier. We then lose sight of Titi. There is no explanation for how it later returns to Ji-young. Similarly, Titi leaves the garage of Tae-hee's house. Again, there is no explanation of how the kitten later ends up back with Tae-hee. The film has given up trying to follow the cat.

One night, both Ji-young and Tae-hee hear Titi's meowing at the same time even though they are in different places. In reality, the two girls may not have heard the cat at all, but parallel editing connecting Ji-young, Titi, and Tae-hee makes us feel that they have. Ji-young wakes up at a juvenile training school and *seemingly* hears something. Titi meows near a window somewhere. Tae-hee silently faces her typewriter, typing something that we do not see. These three shots are placed right next to each other so that we think both Ji-young and Tae-hee hear Titi at the same time. It looks as though Ji-young thinks of something and Tae-hee has made up her mind about something. We never know.

Throughout its history, the city of Incheon has been full of "wanderers," according to director Jeong Jae-eun. Such wanderers include travelers, foreign laborers, and homeless people of various racial, ethnic, and class backgrounds. Incheon is a port city that opened to the outside world in 1883 and was the first city on the Korean Peninsula to encounter the modern cultures of the West. Since then, Incheon has been the center of Korea's industrialization. The city is also known as the site of the Battle of Incheon. In September 1950, during the Korean War, U.S. troops led by General Douglas MacArthur landed at Incheon and conducted a large-scale operation. The 1981 film *Inchon* (Terence Young), produced by the Unification Church, depicted the battle. In this big production, Laurence Olivier played Douglas MacArthur, and the international cast included such big names as Mifune Toshirō and Jacqueline Bissett. In 2001, preceding the 2002 FIFA World Cup co-hosted by South Korea and Japan, Incheon International Airport opened and became the largest airport in South Korea.

There are several scenes that point to Incheon as a cosmopolitan city, where the girls interact with a number of wanderers. Tae-hee and Ji-young distribute leaflets for the sauna at a busy disembarkation port. Most of the people carry luggage and are in a hurry to move on to their next destination. In the chaos, most of the leaflets fall on the ground and are stepped on, ripped, and torn. Even after escaping from the port, Tae-hee and Ji-young are pursued by a scary-looking homeless woman.

Towards the end, the cinematic styles of *Take Care of My Cat* return to different forms of cinematic realism. During the scene at Walmido Island, long takes document the industrial and commercial areas of Incheon along with every step the girls make and every breath they take under the changing light from the sky (Bazinian realism). Then, the girls walk to a bus stop against the strong winds from the ocean, a shot in slow motion. This slow movement is spontaneously connected to the flowing view of the beautiful sunset from the windows of a bus to Seoul. Accompanied by a romantic soundtrack of a male vocalist, dissolving shots keep changing from the industrial scenery of Incheon to the big evening sky, a statue with flying wings that commemorates the one hundredth anniversary of the opening of the port, a highway tunnel, and the big city with its neon lights. This kind of seamless transition of time and space typifies classical Hollywood realism.

In the end, Tae-hee makes up her mind to leave Incheon. She cuts her image out of the gorgeously framed family photo in the living room. Then she takes some money from her father's savings—the supposed salary for her work at the sauna.

The final scene of *Take Care of My Cat* is set in the brand-new Incheon International Airport. Tae-hee heads there with Ji-young, who has just been released from the juvenile training facility. A shot of the two girls walking to the departure lobby suddenly turns into slow motion. The moving image appears about to stop, as if to remind us that this is a story within a film (Brechtian realism).

But in fact, the slow motion never stops. Tae-hee and Ji-young stare forward, take deep breaths, and keep walking. Their movement smoothly dissolves to the movement of an airplane that slowly flies into the big sky. Subtitles appear on the screen: "Good Bye." We do not know where they go and what they have decided. All we know is they are on the go. Remember the words of the director: "I believe that if something is not moving, the energy weakens and it needs to be filled with things that are moving" (Shin 2005, 128).

As a young female filmmaker, Jeong Jae-eun is also trying to keep walking, exploring new possibilities of realism in cinema and reality for young women in South Korea. Good-bye for now, her characters seem to be saying, and good luck.

CHAPTER 8

# Cats Old and New

## Modernity in *Samurai Cat*

*Yamaguchi Yoshitaka and Watanabe Takeshi, Japan, 2014*

## A Film of Shocks

*Samurai Cat* (*Neko zamurai*) is a film of shocks. It is a *jidaigeki* (period drama) film, whose story is set in the premodern period of Japan, that is, before 1868, when the Tokugawa shogunate (feudalist military government) surrendered its rule to the Emperor and the new Meiji government started its modernization and Westernization policy. Most Japanese films have been categorized into two mega-genres: either *jidaigeki* (pre-1868) or *gendaigeki* (post-1868, contemporary drama). *Jidaigeki* as a genre has flourished because samurai swordfights are flashier and more shocking than anything other popular entertainments have to offer.

The protagonist of *Samurai Cat* is Madarame Kyūtarō (Kitamura Kazuki), a *rōnin*, or a samurai who has lost his lord. In the district of Edo where he lives, there are two crime lords, Yonezawa the dog lover and Aikawa the cat lover, competing for supremacy. Because of his renowned sword skill, Kyūtarō is hired by one gangster clan as their *yōjimbō*, or bodyguard. This is a classic plot of *jidaigeki* that calls to mind Akira Kurosawa's famous film *Yojimbo* (*Yōjimbō*, 1961), whose violent but spectacular swordfights shocked not only domestic but international viewers as well, and inspired both *yakuza* (Japanese gangster) films and Spaghetti Westerns.

But the shock of *Samurai Cat* does not come from flashy swordfights. What shocks viewers is that a climactic swordfight, which we anticipate at the film's climax, never happens and our expectation of a *jidaigeki* film is betrayed in a surprising manner. The real shock of the film is a cat, whose encounter with the protagonist persuades the latter to give up his sword.

## The Emergence of *Jidaigeki* in the Period of Modernity

The *jidaigeki* genre emerged in Japan in the 1920s at a time of cultural tur-moil. The period that followed the Great Kanto Earthquake of 1923 witnessed the drastic transformation of Japanese society. Tokyo's rapid reconstruction incorporated urban planning that furthered the modernization and industri-alization begun by the Meiji Restoration. A mass market for films was open-ing up. The number of movie theaters increased rapidly—from 703 in 1923 to 1,013 in 1924—and most were located in urban areas. A working-class culture grew and flourished, and with it labor organization, unionization, and socialist and communist ideas. Popular demand for political participation and democracy resulted in the establishment of a parliamentary government in 1924. Universal suffrage (for men) was promulgated in 1925. This flood of new ideas, from left-wing radicalism to labor unionism, was countered by growing state and military authority, effected by the authoritarian Peace Preservation Law of 1925.

*Jidaigeki* films embraced the tension between democracy and authori-tarianism in their narratives, themes, and styles. In *jidaigeki* films, cinematic styles and techniques were used in a more radical fashion than in other popular films before them. Even though the genre was set in premodern Japan, *jidaigeki* was all about newness. Film critic Takizawa Hajime claims that during the ten years between 1923 and 1932, "*jidaigeki* was more 'modern' than *gendaigeki* [contemporary drama]" (Takizawa 1986, 130).

It is noteworthy that Takizawa used the term "modern" to describe *jidaigeki*. The Oxford English Dictionary defines "modern" as "characteristic of the present time, or the time of writing; not old-fashioned, antiquated, or obsolete; *employing the most up-to-date ideas, techniques, or equipment*." Despite its premodern setting, *jidaigeki* did not depend on premodern styles of enter-tainment. Instead, it employed the "most up-to-date ideas, techniques, or equipment" of the 1920s.

*Jidaigeki* used the techniques of Hollywood cinema extensively to cater to rapidly changing audience tastes, influenced by Western art and popular culture and the speed and spectacle of modern life. The swashbuckling film star Douglas Fairbanks was then the most popular foreign actor in Japan, and *jidaigeki* above all mimicked the athleticism and speed that Fairbanks's films displayed. The swordfights in *jidaigeki,* called *chanbara* to capture the acoustic of swordfights, not only incorporated the continuity editing and crosscut-ting of Hollywood cinema but even went beyond them. In scenes of violent action, the editing became even faster and therefore more shocking than the Hollywood standard, the camera (often handheld) moved swiftly and violently, and fast-motion technique was added. By such methods, *jidaigeki* overcame the slow and static theatricality of *kyūgeki* films (old drama), like those produced earlier in the century by Makino Shōzō, "the father of Japanese cinema."

Even though *kyūgeki* included such cinematic polishes as Méliès-style trick editing and deep space composition to display multiple actions within a frame, it basically reproduced the staged performance of kabuki, a traditional popular theatrical entertainment known for stylized singing, dancing, and acting. *Kyūgeki* imitated kabuki mostly using long shots (a shot taken from a certain distance), long takes (a shot with a long duration), and still frames (no camera movement). Moreover, following kabuki, *kyūgeki* did not use female actors. To viewers who were familiar only with Japanese-made *kyūgeki* films, the styles and techniques of *jidaigeki* were shockingly new.

*Jidaigeki* was also heavily influenced by a brand-new Japanese theatrical art: *shinkokugeki* (new national theater). *Shinkokugeki* was a new school of popular theater founded in 1917 by Sawada Shōjirō and was best known for its realistic, non-stylized, speedy, energetic, and violent swordfights. Most of the *shinkokugeki* repertoires were based on the *jidai shōsetsu* (period novel), the overwhelmingly well-liked *taishū bungaku* (mass literature) genre of popular literature that mainly targeted working-class readers. Realistic swordfights, rather than the dance-like stylized form in kabuki, had a shock value for their audience and were considered to be more suitable to the radical social changes and uncertainties characteristic of the first decades of the twentieth century.

The modern techniques and equipment that enabled the realism of sword-fighting in *shinkokugeki* revolved around lighting. It is unknown whether Sawada was familiar with the work of David Belasco, but the theatrical lighting in *shinkokugeki* was similar to that of Belasco's theater, which, as we saw in Chapter 2 of this book, was heavily influenced by Lasky lighting. In contrast to flat and all-encompassing lighting of kabuki and *kyūgeki,* *jidaigeki* fully incorporated the Belasco-type lighting of *shinkokugeki,* especially with the flash of the sword, both to enhance visual shock and to express complex psychological states of the sword fighters. In *jidaigeki,* characters often wander in the dark. Under the dim moonlight or street lamps, the swords of samurai warriors flash for a moment, as if they cannot wait for bloodshed. Samurai resort to their swords, which embody their spirits, to prove themselves. But they often suffer from the act of killing. The Japanese filmmaker Uratani Toshirō claims, "*Chanbara* is the boiling point where the 'psychological climax' and the 'visual climax' of the drama meet" (Uratani 2004, 24). The Japanese cinematographer Morita Fujio elaborates:

> It has been a regular practice for *tateshi* [the sword-fighting choreographer] to come up with unique sword-fighting methods that could be effectively photographed . . . Psychologically, a bamboo sword transforms into a real sword. It is significant to make the bamboo sword look heavy, edgy, and brutal. It is craftwork to make the sword shine momentarily. The flash emphasizes the fearful nature of the sword especially in close-ups. In this sense, technicians of Daiei studio were extremely sensitive to the environment of sword-fighting scenes. They preferred dawn, dusk, and night to daytime. They liked to juxtapose such natural phenomena as rain or mist with the sense of brutality in sword-fighting. (Morita 2007, 79–80)

Even today, one of the major attractions at Tōei Kyoto Cinema Village, a Universal Studios–style amusement park attached to a film and TV production studio, is a live demonstration of *jidaigeki* filmmaking whose climax is the production of a scene in which a sword flashes in the hands of an actor, reflecting a spotlight. The presenter explains, jokingly, the difficulty and skill required to flash the sword in perfect timing in front of a camera.

It is worth noting that the notion of the samurai's sword embodying his spirit was also one of the new "ideas" employed in Japan during the period of modernization and Westernization. In *Bushido: The Soul of Japan* (1900), Japanese economist and diplomat Nitobe Inazō, referred to the romantic—not necessarily historically accurate—notion that Japanese people had a particular philosophical and moral code called *bushido,* or the code of samurai, handed down through generations. Nitobe wrote, "What [the samurai] carries in his belt is a symbol of what he carries in his mind and heart—loyalty and honour" (Nitobe 2002, 118). Confronting Western imperialism and the rapid Westernization of Japan after the Meiji Restoration, Nitobe strategically emphasized *bushido*—codes of loyalty and filial piety—which he connected to modern Japanese nationalism for his foreign readership. Nitobe claimed, "The samurai grew to be the beau ideal of the whole race . . . Bushido was and still is the animating spirit, the motor force of our country" (Nitobe 2002, 141). Nitobe's tactics might be regarded as an invented tradition that was the forerunner of the self-exoticization policy of the 1950s Japanese film industry and the current governmental policy of "Cool Japan" (see Chapter 6).

Nitobe's tactics worked. By the 1940s, many people had come to believe that the Japanese sword signified the embodiment of the Japanese spirit. The American cultural anthropologist Ruth Benedict juxtaposed the

Japanese sword and the Japanese soul in her classic work, *The Chrysanthemum and the Sword: Patterns of Japanese Culture* (1946). Benedict wrote, "Though every soul originally shines with virtue like a new sword, nevertheless, if it is not kept polished, it gets tarnished. This 'rust of my body,' as they [Japanese people] phrase it, is as bad as it is on a sword. A man must give his character the same care that he would give a sword. But his bright and gleaming soul is still there under the rust and all that is necessary is to polish it up again" (Benedict 1989, 198).

At the end of World War II (see Chapter 5), Japan was under Allied occupation. The occupation government led by General Douglas MacArthur initiated control of the Japanese film industry as a part of its policy of reconstructing Japan. On November 19, 1945, only three months after Japan's surrender to the allied nations, the occupation government made a list of banned topics in films that included militarism, ultranationalism, feudalism, and anything that might be perceived as anti-democratic. Many *jidaigeki* films were banned because of their possible feudal elements (but kissing scenes were recommended as a symbol of American-style liberalism and democracy). The occupational film policy severely controlled *jidaigeki*'s representation of the sword because the sword was regarded as the symbol of the Japanese soul and a possible reference to the upholding of feudalistic loyalty. This is ironic, because originally *jidaigeki* was not so much a "traditional" genre as a "modern" one that was influenced by Hollywood films and by the rebellious genre of *shinkokugeki*. That was why the ultranationalistic militarist government of wartime Japan regulated *jidaigeki* as a Western-style entertainment. Under the occupational film policy, the number of *jidaigeki* released in Japan decreased sharply from 324 (1937) to only two (1945), seven (1946), and eight (1947).

## Vernacular Modernism

The term *modern* and the notion of modernity have been particularly prolific topics of discussion in film studies, especially since film scholar Miriam Bratu Hansen coined the term *vernacular modernism* to describe Hollywood cinema in her influential 1999 essay, "The Mass Production of the Senses: Classical Cinema as Vernacular Modernism." Traditionally, the term *modernism* was defined as an artistic movement prevalent from the late nineteenth century to the first half of the twentieth century. It was an experiment in various fields of cultural production to counter the conventional styles and values. The most noteworthy element was consciousness about the specificity of the medium—its materials and techniques. In the case of modernist cinema, questions included the following: What is cinema? What makes cinema a unique medium? What can cinema do? Avant-garde or experimental film-makers, in particular, explored these questions.

In contrast, Hansen did not discuss modernism in cinema from this type of art-historical context. Instead, she proposed to consider cinema to be a part of the period of modernity. She wrote, "I take the study of modernist aesthetics to encompass cultural practices that both articulated and mediated the experience of modernity, such as the mass-produced and mass-consumed phenomena of fashion, design, advertising, architecture and urban environment, of photography, radio and cinema" (Hansen 1999, 61). Here, Hansen considered modernity to be a combination of changes in the society that included "rapid industrialization, urbanization, and population growth; the proliferation of new technologies and transportations; the saturation of advanced capitalism; the explosion of a mass consumer culture; and so on," and changes of the experience "characterized by the physical and perceptual shocks of the modern urban environment . . . that was markedly quicker, more chaotic, fragmented, and disorienting than in previous phases of human culture" (Singer 2001, 72–73). To Hansen, not just modernist experimental cinema but cinema as a whole formulated and reflected modernity, the culture of shocks. Hollywood cinema, which such scholars as David Bordwell, Kristin Thompson and Janet Steiger have called "classical," had a huge impact in the world film culture because it "produced and globalized" the aesthetics of "vernacular" modernism (Hansen 1999, 72).

*Jidaigeki* of the 1920s certainly embodied the aesthetics of vernacular modernism. The genre simultaneously reflected and formulated the culture of shocks. On the one hand, *jidaigeki* was a "globalized" version of Hollywood swashbuckler films in its techniques and equipment, including lighting technology. On the other hand, as the connection to *shinkokugeki* illustrated, *jidaigeki* also forged its own idioms, such as those that went beyond the Hollywood techniques of continuity editing, even though they were still part of a larger vernacular-modernist culture. In that sense, the relationship between Hollywood and *jidaigeki* was not simply a binary opposition between the production-distribution center and periphery. The relationship was "*at once* cosmopolitan *and* local" (italics in original, Hansen 2010, 291).

## Zorro's Sword, Chūtarō's Sword, Kyūtarō's Sword: To Flash or Not

Douglas Fairbanks's films had a certain impact on the style of *jidaigeki*, but the obsession with the flash of the sword and its symbolic implications distinguished *jidaigeki* from Hollywood swashbuckler films of the same period. The significance of effects lighting was much more enhanced in the swordfights in *jidaigeki*. For instance, in a climactic duel in *Chutaro of Banba: Mother of Memory* (*Banba no Chūtarō: Mabuta no haha,* Inagaki Hiroshi, 1931), the swords shine spectacularly. After defeating his enemies, Chūtarō, played by the *jidaigeki* star Kataoka Chiezō, throws away his sword. It sticks into the bottom of a tree and shines conspicuously white. Then the camera slowly pans to the right until it captures Chūtarō and his mother, for whom he has been searching a long time, embracing each other and sobbing. While they were separated, Chūtarō was forced out of necessity to become a hired swordsman.

This finale was surely inspired by the ending of *The Mark of Zorro* (Fred Niblo, 1920), a Douglas Fairbanks star vehicle that was popularly received in Japan. When Zorro, played by Fairbanks, throws away his sword after the climactic battle, it sticks into the wall. In the following long shot, Zorro jumps up to the second floor. Then, in the following medium long shot, Zorro and his sweetheart embrace each other. However, Zorro's sword does not conspicuously shine as it quivers, pinned to the wall. While both Chūtarō and Zorro decide to give up their swords and most likely their professions as swordsmen, lighting illustrates the different significance that act holds for each of them. For Zorro, the sword does not have much of an impact on his life, but for Chūtarō, the sword is his soul. Chūtarō is in tears not only of joy in reuniting with his mother but also of dismay at his identity crisis.

In *Samurai Cat,* Kyūtarō, whose name reminds us of Chūtarō, similarly gives up his sword when the climactic battle between the Yonezawa gang and the Aikawa gang is about to begin. Unlike Chūtarō's sword, however, his does not flash or shine at all. When the enemy bodyguard challenges Kyūtarō to a duel, Kyūtarō draws his sword in response. But his sword goes out of the frame so quickly that we cannot even see it clearly. We the viewers wonder for a little while where the sword has gone. Then, in the following long shot, we see it stuck firmly into the ground. The publicity photo of this scene displays Kyūtarō holding a cat, Tamanojō, in his left arm and preparing for the enemy attack with a shining sword in his right hand. This is an iconic image of a *jidaigeki* samurai (except for the cat). Yet the film does not emphasize this fighting pose. Instead, the audience notices how, under the dull daylight, Kyūtarō's sword does not reflect any light to make it conspicuously shine. Kyūtarō rejects the challenge and declares that he will not use his sword. Impressed by his conviction, the enemy bodyguard withdraws his challenge and sheaths his sword. The two gang bosses witness the scene as well, and they make peace. Kyūtarō's nonviolent but disobedient tactic succeeds.

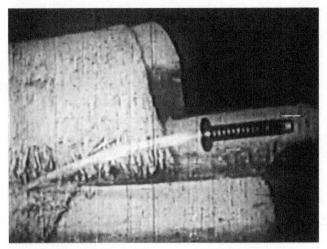

Chūtarō's sword shines.

Zorro's sword pinned to the wall, not shining.

It is noteworthy that in *Samurai Cat* Kyūtarō never depends on his sword to verify his identity. Yes, we are told that he has a masterful technique that made him a swordfight instructor in Kaga, his hometown. But there is no scene in this *jidaigeki* film in which he kills a person with his sword. We also never see his sword flash spectacularly. For him, the sword is not his soul. Instead, we find that Kyūtarō was once fired from his position in Kaga because he was not able to use his sword to assist his fellow samurai in committing hara-kiri. He became *rōnin* and came to Edo to find a job

Kyūtarō's sword stuck into the ground, not shining.

as a samurai. In other words, he has tried to make his sword his soul, his identity, especially to gain respectability and for his wife and daughter, but he ultimately fails.

In this sense, *Samurai Cat* is an anti-*jidaigeki*. It rejects the shock of swordfights. It forswears the spectacle of the shining weapon. It maintains only the rebellious idea of rebellion against the dominant mode of expression that *jidaigeki* had in the 1920s against kabuki and *kyūgeki*. It is notable, though, to see a samurai giving up his weapon if we consider the current right-wing political trend in Japan, led by Prime Minister Abe Shinzō. In July 2014, the Abe cabinet decided to reinterpret the national Constitution of Japan, whose Article 9 outlaws war as a means to settle international disputes involving the state, and to allow for the right of "Collective Self-Defense." This would allow the Japan Self-Defense Forces to aid allied nations under attack. Despite public backlash, the "Peace and Security Preservation Legislation" bills that Abe's cabinet introduced to the Diet were approved in September 2015. The nonviolent tactics adopted by Kyūtarō, which implicitly go against government policy regarding the Self-Defense Forces, may have been possible because *Samurai Cat* was not produced by one of the major broadcasting networks in Japan but by Tō-Mei-Han Net 6 and 5 Issho 3 Channel, which are members of the Japanese Association of Independent Television Stations. First produced as a TV series in October 2013, its steady popularity led to the production and release of the film version. As if to challenge Prime Minister Abe's policy-making, season two of the TV series appeared from April to June 2015 and a sequel, *Samurai Cat 2: A Tropical Adventure* (*Neko zamurai 2: Minami no shima e iku,* Watanabe Takeshi), was released in September 2015.

## The Unpredictable Nature of the Cat

Even if *Samurai Cat* does not have any flashy swordfights, it is still a film of shocks in a visual sense. Instead of the sword, various cinematic techniques, including lighting, framing, and editing, are adopted to make the cat, Tamanojō, stand out.

The cat's eyes and fur shine in particular scenes. As the hired bodyguard of Yonezawa's dog-loving gang, Kyūtarō is asked to kill Tamanojō, the beloved cat of the boss, Aikawa. Tamanojō is also wanted by a magistrate to mate with his cat. The connection between Aikawa and the magistrate threatens to damage Yonezawa. One dark night, Kyūtarō sneaks into the house of the cat-loving Aikawa clan. Low-key lighting is adopted throughout this scene in order to create a chiaroscuro effect and to heighten the suspenseful mood. The visible sources of lighting are the moon for the exterior shots and candles and traditional paper lanterns for the interior shots. Especially after Kyūtarō goes into Tamanojō's room, the candle flames and the paper lanterns are the only bright spots around Kyūtarō. The camera zooms into a medium close-up of Kyūtarō, who now makes a grimace and raises his sword. He is surrounded by darkness.

Then suddenly, the shot is reversed to a close-up of Tamanojō the cat, who turns her face to the right. Her eyes hold the bright light and her fur shines in an angelic manner. Despite the dark surroundings, three-point-lighting is adopted to enhance her appeal, especially in Kyūtarō's eyes. (Remember our discussion of three-point lighting, which enhances the attraction of the heroine in the shadowy room near the opening of *Cat People*.) This is a visual shock to Kyūtarō; he is helpless before Tamanojō, whose beauty is enhanced by lighting and framing. It is love at first sight,

Tamanojō in three-point lighting.

and Kyūtarō surrenders unconditionally. Kyūtarō kidnaps Tamanojō after making it appear that he has killed her.

A second technique in filming the cat is to make it appear and reappear in unexpected places at unexpected moments. Even though Kyūtarō has brought Tamanojō into his home, he is shocked by her behaviors again and again. Framing is effectively used to depict Kyūtarō's futile efforts to keep her away from his side business of making paper umbrellas. Every time Kyūtarō carries Tamanojō out of the frame, she comes back on screen to disrupt his work. Exhausted, Kyūtarō decides to dump Tamanojō. He leaves her in the woods but begins to worry about her when rain starts to fall. When he wakes up in the middle of the night, he finds Tamanojō right next to his bed, drenched. No explanation is given for her return. Tamanojō just reappears. Kyūtarō begins to dry her with a cloth. The medium close-up emphasizes the first direct kinship between the samurai and the cat.

The techniques of flashback and voiceover are also prominently used in *Samurai Cat*. Flashback and voiceover are considered the signature techniques of film noir (as seen in Chapter 5). In film noir, a paranoiac male protagonist often remembers his past in a subjective manner with the help of flashback and voiceover. In most cases, he regrets what has happened to him, especially after meeting a femme fatale (literally, a woman of fate).

Kyūtarō keeps remembering his past: how he lost his position as swordfight instructor in Kaga and how he left his wife and daughter. It is a traumatic memory for him, and he habitually speaks to himself of his feelings and thoughts. Despite its extensive use of flashback and voiceover and the presence of the paranoiac protagonist, however, *Samurai Cat* is not a film noir. Even though Kyūtarō meets a "woman" of fate, Tamanojō is not a femme fatale. Yes, the encounter with her might have been the most

The kinship between the samurai and the cat.

shocking thing in his life. His daily life has changed because of her, and now it is difficult for him to maintain his side business; he needs to learn how to feed a cat, etc. Yet, Tamanojō does not really transform Kyūtarō. Even before he met her, Kyūtarō could not use his sword to kill people. He tries to change his attitude to fit with the ideal image of a samurai, or *bushido*, but is not successful. The shock of the cat only confirms his belief in nonviolence. In the end, he simply goes home to his family, with the cat. The sword as a weapon does not matter to Kyūtarō from the beginning to the end.

## Cats Are Modern

Even if Tamanojō does not change Kyūtarō's identity, she shakes up his world. As we have seen, the cinematic techniques in *Samurai Cat* are used to enhance the shocking effect of the cat. In fact, like the swords in *jidaigeki*, cats have represented the culture of modernity. Film scholar Rosalind Galt writes, "[I]n the age of photography cats take on a new cultural role, their bodies used to figure modernity's themes of movement and the street. We see the effects of this shift in the elegant cat silhouettes of Manet but its direct appearance is in cinema, where the new figurability of unpredictable feline motion articulates the close affinity of cats to the discourses of cinematic modernity" (Galt 2015, 43).

We discussed in Chapter 6 that cats played a significant role in nineteenth-century art as painters tried to capture their movements. *Hokusai Manga,* a woodblock-printed collection of sketches of various subjects including cats by the *ukiyo-e* artist Katsushika Hokusai, had a huge impact on Impressionist painters in Europe. The work of Édouard Manet to which Galt refers was produced under that influence. Beyond *Hokusai Manga,* the images of cats were one of the forerunners of the culture of modernity, fast-paced consumer culture in particular, in Japan.

It is said that another *ukiyo-e* artist, Utagawa Kuniyoshi (1798–1861), initiated the first boom of cats in popular culture in Japan. Being a cat lover, Kuniyoshi illustrated famous kabuki actors in cat form. This was Kuniyoshi's playful strategy to avoid censorship during the early 1840s that banned representations of kabuki actors, courtesans, and geisha as the symbols of luxury and of subversive ideas (Kennedy, n.p.). Yet, Kuniyoshi's *ukiyo-e* prints with cats became hugely popular. Woodblock printing marked the start of literary mass production in Japan in the seventeenth and eighteenth centuries, and its product, *ukiyo-e,* became mass-marketed, especially among the merchant class, or the nouveaux riches. By the mid-nineteenth century, total circulation of a print could run into the thousands (Ōkubo 2008,

153–154). In addition, Kuniyoshi's prints of cats had another function in the industrialization of Japan. During the Edo period, sericulture (silk production) became an important Japanese industry. Cats were widely used to protect the silkworms from mice. But many cats were imported from China, and their number was limited. Merchants who could not obtain actual cats used Kuniyoshi's prints as amulets.

Thus, in the late nineteenth and early twentieth centuries, cats' "unpredictable" quick movements were suitable subjects of cinema. I referred to Edison's *The Boxing Cat* (1894) in the introduction of this book. I have also mentioned that the Lumière brothers, Edison's rivals, also produced at least seven films with cats between 1896 and 1900. One of them is called *The Little Girl and Her Cat* (*La Petite fille et son chat,* 1900). This less-than-one-minute film captures a little girl (Madeline Koehler) and a black cat in one shot, a medium close-up. Sitting on a chair with small table, she feeds the cat ten times from her extended right arm. The cat suddenly gets distracted and jumps off to the right after the third feeding. Then, the cat quickly jumps back from outside of the frame and reaches its paw to the girl's hand to grab the food (the eighth and tenth times). Rosalind Galt makes this point about the film:

> As relatively untrainable animals, cats can't be relied upon to do what the film-maker wants. Even a pet cat being bribed with copious amounts of food is just as likely to notice something interesting elsewhere and leave, and so a cute actuality about a little girl and her cat becomes a narrative about on- and off-screen space, about desire, about the unpredictable; in short, about unbiddable life. (Galt 2015, 43)

In reality, it is very difficult to make cats eat against their will, or to make them perform during the actual shooting of films. *Day for Night* (*La Nuit américaine,* François Truffaut, 1973) is a film about film production. There is a scene in which the crew has a hard time getting a cat to drink milk. A cat trainer remarks that this is strange because he has not fed the cat for two days. I myself once tried to film my cat when I made a student film. It did not work at all because my cat was so distracted by people and cars on the street that it was nearly impossible to capture her image within the camera frame. I tried to give her some food and treats to soothe her, but it was no use. The unpredictable nature of cats was thus revealed during the production of *Samurai Cat* as well as during the production of my own film.

Thus, Tamanojō is much more volatile than the sword in *jidaigeki*. She is modern.

# Cats Like Watching

## History in *The Cats of Mirikitani*

*Linda Hattendorf, USA/Japan, 2006*

### *The Cats of Mirikitani* and the Cat of Linda

*The Cats of Mirikitani,* a documentary, begins like a boy-meets-girl film. Linda Hattendorf, the director of the film, lives in an apartment in Soho, New York, with her cat. The tortoiseshell is a little overweight, but her fur is beautiful and her eyes are sparkling. She must be well taken care of. There is an elderly homeless man on the sidewalk in front of Linda's neighborhood deli. He often paints pictures of cats. If Linda were not a cat lover, she might not have noticed him. Since she is a cat person, she becomes interested in the elderly painter. That is, Linda and Jimmy Mirikitani meet thanks to cats.

Eight months later, 9/11 occurs. The World Trade Center collapses, and Lower Manhattan is evacuated. Jimmy has no place to go, and Linda takes him into her apartment. Cats usually do not like intruders—either other cats or strangers—in their territories. But Linda's cat accepts Jimmy rather naturally. Sitting in front of a TV with Jimmy, the cat looks at the images of the collapsing twin towers, of George W. Bush addressing the American people, of air raids in Afghanistan, of attacks on Arab markets in New York, of people questioning Islam within the United States. Jimmy murmurs, "It is the same as old days." In this scene, a close-up of Linda's cat gazing at something is inserted so that Jimmy and the images on the TV seem to be watched from the cat's perspective (POV editing).

Cats like watching, indeed. As film scholar Rosalind Galt writes, "cats do watch moving images" with "avid engagement" (Galt 2015, 48). Every evening, when I watch a film on TV, my cat is lying on a sofa right next to me and quietly looking at the TV screen. Galt claims, "Cats certainly don't

Close-up of Linda's cat.

The scene on the TV screen.

understand the concept of representation, but they can process representational images" (Galt 2015, 50). While Galt's cat "only watches animal shows on television and leaves in boredom if she sees too many shots of human presenters" (Galt 2015, 50), my cat seems to keep watching the screen shimmering in black and white. Most of the time I watch black and white films, so my cat may not "process representational images" but simply be gazing at presented images. But in the film, because of POV editing, we feel that Linda's cat is actually processing the images represented on the TV screen along with Jimmy.

When Linda was filming for *The Cats of Mirikitani,* she was also continuing her daily job and was not at home during the day. So the director decided to leave the camera at home to capture Jimmy, who was absorbed by his painting in the apartment. In the film, standing with his round shoulders (*neko-ze,* or "cat's shoulders," in Japanese), Jimmy faces a big sheet of paper on a table. He sings Japanese children's songs and popular ballads as he paints. It looks as if the cat, who also stays at the apartment, is recording Jimmy's activities. (In reality, though, the camera might have been operated by Masa Yoshikawa, who is also credited as a cinematographer of this film.) The cat records Jimmy's paintings, including a picture of a cat comfortably sleeping right next to ripe red persimmons from Hiroshima; a picture of red carp (the baseball team in Hiroshima is the Carp); a picture of the World Trade Center on fire; and a picture of the Atomic Bomb Dome in Hiroshima on fire. Jimmy lost his family members and friends to the atomic bomb. The color red connects persimmons, carp, and fire. The images of war give way to those of cats mischievously looking at the carp or taking a nap right next to the persimmons. "War is bad," Jimmy mutters.

Jimmy keeps painting pictures of cats even after moving into Linda's apartment. But they are not sketches of Linda's tortoiseshell. Are they cats from his memories? Did he have cats in those "old days"?

Showing his paintings and his old photos to Linda, Jimmy starts to talk about his past little by little. He was born in Sacramento, California, so he has US citizenship. When he was three, his mother took him to Hiroshima, where he became interested in ink painting. He returned to the United States when he was eighteen and started working in Oakland, California.

Jimmy Mirikitani draws a picture of a cat.

Shortly after he moved to Seattle, the Japanese attacked Pearl Harbor, and the war between the US and Japan began.

In 1942, because of Franklin D. Roosevelt's Executive Order 9066, he was relocated to an internment camp in Tule Lake at the border between California and Oregon. He was forced to give up his US citizenship there. Conditions in the camp were horrible, and many people died there. At Tule Lake, Jimmy met a boy who was fond of cats. Pets were not allowed at internment camps, and he was not able to bring his cat there. The boy asked Jimmy, who was a good painter, "Brother, paint a picture of a Japanese cat." Ever since, Jimmy has painted pictures of cats. For the boy. In order not to forget the history of the internment camp, and the boy who did not leave the camp alive. The cats of Mirikitani—they are cats that remember.

"To articulate what is past does not mean to recognize 'how it really was,'" wrote philosopher Walter Benjamin in his 1940 essay "On the Concept of History." It means to hold fast "to a picture of the past, just as if it had unexpectedly thrust itself, in a moment of danger, on the historical subject." On 9/11, "a moment of danger," a memory of the internment camp "thrust itself" onto Jimmy Mirikitani, and Jimmy could not help murmuring, "It is the same as old days." Benjamin imagined an "Angel of History," its face turned towards the past, pausing "to awaken the dead and to piece together what has been smashed." The cats of Mirikitani may represent that angel.

## Cinema, History, and Viewing Positions

In his book *Cinema and History,* film scholar Mike Chopra-Gant suggests that cinema can be a form of evidence of the social values and discourses predominant during the historical moment in which it is produced (Chopra-Gant 2008, 11–28). In other words, cinema is a historical document. This does not simply mean that the content of cinema reflects society, but that it exists in society and is produced and received within the complex network of people who are living in that society.

This issue has become evident along with the development of reception studies in film studies. In addition to analyzing films as aesthetic and symbolic audiovisual texts, which presupposes a theoretical and often passive spectator, reception studies explores diverse ways of reading films depending on the viewers' positions. In previous chapters, I have often used "we" or "viewers" when I describe people who watch films. I may have been too general. For the convenience of my arguments, I may have taken a certain viewing position—emotional, psychological, or interpretive—for granted. I may have reduced multiple possible perspectives to only one. It is convenient to regard viewers as a single entity, but we need to be careful when we do so.

Thanks to the development of videos, DVDs, satellite TV, cable TV, and the internet, the space for watching films has gone beyond movie theaters and expanded to personal TVs, computer screens, tablets, and cell phones. Under such conditions, it is difficult to assume a particular viewing position. Moreover, I belong to a certain social group that is different from yours in terms of race, ethnicity, nationality, class, gender, age, occupation, interests, and so on. Given all this, we cannot simply say "we the viewers."

The reception of *The Cats of Mirikitani,* as a historical document, has been diverse, depending on the viewers' positions. Here is how I viewed it, from my position as a non-US citizen living in New York in 2001 at a time when I was engrossed in my dissertation on a particular historical moment in early twentieth-century cinema history.

## The Cat of Miyao

On the morning of September 11, I sat facing my laptop in a small studio apartment in Brooklyn. When I happened to glance up, I noticed my cat sitting beside the window, looking outside and listening. A radio from the street blared louder than usual, and I heard the words "hijack" and "state of emergency." Suddenly alert, I turned on the TV. Like so many others, I could not believe what I saw. It looked like a Hollywood film (perhaps the final scene of *Fight Club* [David Fincher, 1999] starring Brad Pitt). But when I stepped out of my apartment and turned my eyes toward Manhattan,

The author's cat poses for the camera.

a huge plume of gray smoke was rising. As it slowly approached Brooklyn like a cloud, I could no longer think that the scene before me looked like a film. It was reality.

Like Jimmy, I experienced 9/11 as a "moment of danger." I had never been sent to an internment camp, but my dissertation research examined anti-Japanese sentiment in the 1920s, a time when the term "Yellow Peril" was prevalent and a recent act of the US Congress had targeted Japanese immigrants by prohibiting the entry of "aliens ineligible for citizenship." As I gazed at the smoke, it was easy to envision that same kind of racism rising up to cloud the lives of a different group of immigrants.

When 9/11 occurred, Jimmy shut himself up in Linda's apartment with her cat and grew more absorbed in his painting, as if he were trying to capture the "picture of the past" of himself as a racial minority in the US. So did I. I confined myself to my apartment and focused on writing my dissertation as if I were trying to grasp the "picture of the past," of Japanese people in the US as a racial minority, by way of cinema, or pictures of the past. Linda continued her research in order to record Jimmy's memory as history. I, too, continued my research so that I could understand the history of racism that had existed before the internment camps. As such, I reacted to the film *The Cats of Mirikitani* collectively as a member of a minority group living in the US.

## The Cats of Mirikitani Reborn

Mike Chopra-Gant suggests that cinema not only represents a historical moment, but also creates narratives of the past (Chopra-Gant 51–69). In other words, and especially in the case of historical dramas, such as *The Birth of a Nation* (D. W. Griffith, 1915), cinema tells a (hi)story. Authenticity, historical truth, and objectivity are always subjects of debate in such films. *The Birth of a Nation* was perceived by many as an authentic depiction of the history of the US Civil War when the film was initially released, despite the film's racist content and its glorification of the KKK. (The story of *The Birth of a Nation* focuses on two families: one from the North and the other from the South. Both families own cats, and the heroine, played by Lillian Gish, first appears with a white cat.)

In addition to representing the historical moment of 2001, *The Cats of Mirikitani* also creates a narrative. The film tells a personal history of Jimmy Mirikitani from his perspective. In real life as well as within the storyline of this documentary, director Linda Hattendorf conducts her own archival research to support Jimmy's story with empirical evidence. In that sense, this film tells the story of Linda's proactive attempt to restore the years that Jimmy lost in the history of World War II and afterward.

In the film, Linda contacts the Social Security office because she wants to help Jimmy. She does not want to leave him on the streets, which are now filled with dust from the World Trade Center collapse, but she cannot have him in her apartment forever. According to Jimmy, he came to New York a few years after he was released from the internment camp. He worked at restaurants, cooked for Jackson Pollock, and then was hired as a live-in chef at a luxurious apartment on Park Avenue. If so, he had jobs until he became homeless in the 1980s, and, Linda reasons, he must have paid Social Security tax. But Jimmy stubbornly rejects the support that the people at Social Security offer. He says he does not want any help from the United States. Why does he decline their support so persistently?

Linda continues her online research in order to record a "picture of the past" that "had unexpectedly thrust itself" onto Jimmy Mirikitani and secure it as history. She finds out that Jimmy himself made efforts after the war to recover his citizenship. He sent letters to the US government a number of times and asked for his American citizenship back because he had a dream of working as a painter and becoming a bridge between East and West. But he never received any response from America. He feels that he can no longer trust the Social Security office even if they now offer their support. It is too late.

In fact, the US government sent him a letter in 1959. Jimmy kept moving, however, so the letter was returned to the sender. Jimmy's citizenship had in fact been restored decades ago. He just didn't know it. Linda's research has had an unexpected result. Jimmy's closed heart starts to open. He is invited as a guest instructor to a painting class for elderly people at the Social Security office. He paints a picture of a cat. Participants are amazed at how Jimmy completes the picture of a cute cat in only a couple of minutes. Jimmy bashfully reports to Linda, "They said to me, 'Teacher, please teach to us [sic] again.'"

Led by cats, Linda met Jimmy and had a chance to see a "picture of the past" in "a moment of danger" of 9/11 and documented the historical moment. Led by cats, Jimmy met Linda and had a chance to face a "picture of the past" in "a moment of danger" and recollect his history. Moreover, Jimmy and Linda created their own narrative to (re)write the history of a Japanese-American person with this film, *The Cats of Mirikitani*. The cat that Jimmy painted with black ink looks as though it is smiling now.

## The Cat of Miyatake

*The Period that Toyo Miyatake Looked into* (*Tōyō Miyatake ga nozoita jidai,* 2008) is another documentary about the Japanese internment experience. Directed by Suzuki Junichi, it is a filmic attempt to re-document a historical moment recorded by Toyo Miyatake (1896–1979), a professional photographer who, like Jimmy Mirikitani, was interned in 1941 (but at Manzanar rather than Tule Lake). Miyatake secretly brought along a lens, and once inside the camp made a camera and started taking pictures. Then, the head of the camp officially asked Miyatake to photograph the camp. Suzuki's documentary had a goal similar to Linda Hattendorf's: while Hattendorf rerecorded the past that Jimmy Mirikitani had captured in his paintings of cats, Suzuki documented the historical moment that Miyatake captured in his photographs.

Before being sent to the camp, Miyatake's photography was famous for its aesthetic use of contrast between light and shadow as well as its abstract composition of nature and human beings. It was art photography. However, at the camp, Miyatake focused on recording history. Obsessed with details, he captured buildings, furniture, and Japanese rituals. He treated Japanese people collectively as a group with a unique culture. He bet on the camera's capability of mechanical reproduction, the realism that André Bazin valued so highly. Miyatake said to his son, "It is a photographer's duty to record the facts that must not be repeated with his camera."

Critic Andreas Hyussen wrote in *Twilight Memories: Marking Time in a Culture of Amnesia* (1994), "The past is not simply there in memory, but it must be articulated to become memory" (Hyussen 1994, 3). Both Jimmy's paintings of cats and Miyatake's photos of the camp were methods of articulation in order to document the past. Both films, *The Cats of Mirikitani* and *The Period that Toyo Miyatake Looked into,* recapture such attempts to document the historical moments of the 1940s and tell the stories in the 2000s.

Curiously, both works resort to cats to narrate their (hi)stories. When his documentary film was released, Suzuki published a picture book with his wife, actor Sakakibara Rumi. The book, *Uncle Toyo's Camera: Photographer Toyo Miyatake and Japanese People in America during the War* (*Tōyō ojisan no kamera: Shashinka Miyatake Tōyō to senjika no zaibei nikkeijin tachi*) is about Miyatake's experiences at the internment camp in Manzanar seen from a cat's point of view. A stray cat becomes lost and ends up inside the camp in Manzanar. Miyatake finds the cat and names it Miew. Miew looks at people's lives in the camp and is a witness to the results of the racist policies that sent American citizens there. Miew also feels the suffering of the Nisei who decide to fight against Japan, where their families came from.

There is no record that Miyatake ever had a cat in the camp. No one was allowed to bring pets to the camps. Why, then, did Suzuki use a cat as the narrator of his story? Perhaps his picture book required a cute, relatable character for its young readers. Or perhaps the cat is a symbol of free will. Despite the big sky and the land around them, Japanese internees are confined in a camp surrounded by barbed wire. Miew says to herself, "I can go out if I want . . ." The cat may represent both the hope and the despair of the people in the camp as they yearn for freedom.

But the most important reason may be that cats are creatures who watch. Just like Benjamin's Angel of History, cats have always been watching us, and they will continue to do so.

# Glossary

180-degree rule: The initial shot of a scene draws an imaginary line, called the axis of action, which divides the action space in two halves. The first is where the camera is located, while the second is on the other side of that line. This setup allows the camera position to be varied between shots, as long as the centerline is not crossed. Once a camera is placed, it must stay on the same side and cannot cross the axis of action in the scene.

Aspect ratio: The relationship between the width and height of the frame. It includes 1.33: 1 (standard), 1.85: 1 (widescreen), or 2.66: 1 (CinemaScope).

Close-up: A shot in which the camera tightly frames an object or a human face. When the camera moves even closer, the shot is called extreme close-up.

Crosscutting: An editing technique that establishes actions occurring at the same time. For instance, the camera captures two running people in two separate shots. If the camera cuts away from one action to the other and show these two shots by turns, one seems to be chasing the other even though the two are never in the same shot together.

Continuity editing: An editing style that has been adopted by mainstream Hollywood cinema. Filmmaker D. W. Griffith, "the father of Hollywood cinema," developed continuity editing in the 1910s with the goal of creating a universal language of cinema for audiences of all classes all over the world. Such editing techniques as the 180-degree rule, crosscutting, and POV editing (*see* POV) are examples of continuity editing. The focus of continuity editing is to formulate a smooth and seamless narrative development for viewers.

Deep focus: Also known as depth of field. Everything visible within a frame is in focus.

Diegetic sound: The source of the sound is visible or implied in the scene. See also Voiceover.

Flashback: A character recollects what happened to him or her in the past. The plot moves back and shows events that took place before the current one. The beginning of a flashback is often indicated by a close-up of the character who recollects the past.

Gaze: The term "gaze" was first popularized in the 1960s by psychoanalyst Jacques Lacan to describe the anxious state when one becomes aware that she or he is viewed and feels that she or he loses autonomy and turns into an object. Film theorist Laura Mulvey introduced the concept of the "male gaze" and pointed out that mainstream films, particularly Hollywood films, naturalize conventional gender relations in which the figure of woman functions as the object of male desire.

High-angle shot: A shot in which the camera looks down.

High-key lighting. The overall tone of a shot is bright, and the contrast between bright and dark area is minimal.

Intellectual montage: An editing technique that combines two shots with different images that do not have any obvious connection. Their collision brings about new meanings, complex concepts, or even subjective messages that cannot be expressed by each individual image. Soviet filmmaker Sergei Eisenstein came up with this idea of intellectual montage while examining hieroglyphs and Chinese and Japanese languages and characters.

Lasky lighting: In this lighting scheme, as in a Rembrandt painting, a spotlight is directed to a limited area within a frame, which not only creates clear shadows but also indicates the source and direction of light. Director Cecil B. DeMille and his cinematographer Alvin Wyckoff, who developed this lighting style around 1915, had contracts with the Jesse L. Lasky Feature Play Company at that time, hence the term Lasky lighting.

Long shot: A shot size that typically shows the entire object or human body. When the camera moves back further, the shot is called an extreme long shot.

Long take: A shot with long duration. In a long take, time flows continuously as in the real world because there is no cut in the middle.

Low-angle shot: A shot in which the camera looks up.

Low-key lighting: The overall tone of a shot is dark, and the contrast between light and dark is strong.

Medium shot: A shot in which the camera frames a human figure from the waist up. This is also called a waist shot.

Non-diegetic sound: The source of the sound is not visible or implied in the scene.

POV (point of view) editing: A shot taken from a camera that is placed at the height of a character's eyes. A close-up or a medium shot of the character looking at something off-screen is placed before and/or after the first shot. This gives the viewer the impression that the first shot is what the character is looking at. This combination of shots, which creates the sense of a character's view, is called POV editing. The initial shot is called the POV shot.

Shot: An uninterrupted image taken by a camera.

Shot reverse shot: A technique in which one character is shown looking at another character in one shot, and then in the following shot the other character is shown looking back at the first character.

Three-point lighting: A lighting scheme that consists of three lights—key light, fill light, and backlight. The key light brings the primary light to the subject and highlights the form and dimension of it. The fill light, usually a soft and indirect supplementary light that does not change the character of the key light, is used to erase darkly shaded areas on the subject. The backlight, which is placed behind the subject at a slightly higher angle in order not to be seen by the camera, distinguishes the subject from its background and provides a sense of three-dimensionality.

Voiceover: A narration, usually not accompanied by the image of the character himself or herself in the shot (*see also* non-diegetic sound *and* diegetic sound).

# Filmography

*American in Paris, An* (Vincent Minnelli, 1951)
*Ants* (*Ari-chan,* Seo Mitsuyo, 1941)
*Avatar* (James Cameron, 2009)
*Ball at the Anjo House, The* (*Anjō ke no butōkai,* Yoshimura Kōzaburō, 1947)
*Bambi* (David Hand, James Algar, Bill Roberts, Norman Wright, Samuel Armstrong,
    Paul Satterfield, Graham Heid, 1942)
*Battleship Potemkin* (Sergei Eisenstein, 1925)
*Big Sleep, The* (Howard Hawks, 1946)
*Birth of a Nation, The* (D. W. Griffith, 1915)
*Black Cat Mansion* (*Bōrei kaibyō yashiki,* Nakagawa Nobuo, 1958)
*Blade Runner* (Ridley Scott, 1982)
*Blonde Venus* (Josef von Sternberg, 1932)
*Blue Angel, The (Der blau Engel,* Josef von Sternberg, 1930)
*Boxing Cats, The* (Thomas Edison, 1894)
*Breakfast at Tiffany's* (Blake Edwards, 1961)
*Bringing Up Baby* (Howard Hawks, 1938)
*Casablanca* (Michael Curtiz, 1942)
*Cat People* (Jacques Tourneur, 1942)
*Cats of Mirikitani, The* (Linda Hattendorf, 2006)
*Cheat, The* (Cecil B. DeMille, 1915)
*Children's Hour, The* (William Wyler, 1961)
*Chutaro of Banba: Mother of Memory* (*Banba no Chūtarō: Mabuta no haha,* Inagaki
    Hiroshi, 1931)
*Citizen Kane* (Orson Welles, 1940)
*Crucified Lovers, The* (*Chikamatsu monogatari,* Mizoguchi Kenji, 1954)
*Dark Night's Passing, A* (*An'ya kōro,* Toyoda Shirō, 1959)
*Day for Night* (*La Nuit américaine,* François Truffaut, 1973)
*Devil Is a Woman, The* (Josef von Sternberg, 1935)
*Dishonored* (Josef von Sternberg, 1931)

*Don't Bother to Knock* (Roy Ward Baker, 1952)
*Double Indemnity* (Billy Wilder, 1944)
*Female Genealogy* (*Onna keizu*, Makino Masahiro, 1942)
*Fight Club* (David Fincher, 1999)
*Galaxy Express* 999 (Ginga *tetsudō 999*, Rintarō, 1979)
*Gate of Hell* (*Jigokumon*, Kinugasa Teinosuke, 1954)
*Ghost Cat of Otama Pond* (*Kaibyō Otamagaike*, Ishikawa Yoshirō, 1960)
*Ghost of Saga Mansion* (*Kaidan Saga yashiki*, Arai Ryōhei, 1953)
*Godfather, The* (Francis Ford Coppola, 1972)
*Great Train Robbery, The* (Edwin S. Porter, 1903)
*I Am a Cat* (*Wagahai wa neko dearu*, Ichikawa Kon, 1975)
*Inchon* (Terence Young, 1981)
*Jungle Emperor Leo* (*Janguru taitei*, Takeuchi Yoshio, 1997)
*La Bête humaine* (Jean Renoir, 1938)
*Lady from Shanghai, The* (Orson Welles, 1948)
*Lady in the Lake* (Robert Montgomery, 1947)
*Laura* (Otto Preminger, 1944)
*Lion King, The* (Roger Allers and Rob Minkoff, 1994)
*Little Girl and Her Cat, The* (*La Petite fille et son chat*, director unknown, 1900)
*Love of Actress Sumako, The* (*Joyū Sumako no koi*, Mizoguchi Kenji, 1947)
*Magnificent Ambersons, The* (Orson Welles, 1942)
*Maltese Falcon, The* (John Huston, 1941)
*Mark of Zorro, The* (Fred Niblo, 1920)
*Morocco* (Josef von Sternberg, 1930)
*No Regrets for Our Youth* (*Waga seishun ni kui nashi*, Kurosawa Akira, 1946)
*North by Northwest* (Alfred Hitchcock, 1959)
*Osaka Elegy* (*Naniwa erejī*, Mizoguchi Kenji, 1936)
*Out of the Past* (Jacques Tourneur, 1947)
*Pawnbroker, The* (Sydney Lumet, 1964)
*Peachboy's Sea-eagle* (*Momotarō no umiwashi*, Seo Mitsuyo, 1943)
*Period that Toyo Miyatake Looked into, The* (*Tōyō Miyatake ga nozoita jidai*, Suzuki
    Junichi, 2008)
*Pink Panther, The* (Blake Edwards, 1963)
*Port of Shadows, The* (*Le Quai des brumes*, Marcel Carné, 1938)
*Private Life of a Cat, The* (Alexander Hammid and Maya Deren, 1944)
*Rashomon* (*Rashōmon*, Kurosawa Akira, 1950)
*Roman Holiday* (William Wyler, 1953)
*Rope* (Alfred Hitchcock, 1948)
*Sabrina* (Billy Wilder, 1954)
*Samurai Cat* (*Neko zamurai*, Yamaguchi Yoshitaka and Watanabe Takeshi, 2014)
*Samurai Cat 2: A Tropical Adventure* (*Neko zamurai 2: Minami no shima e iku*,
    Watanabe Takeshi, 2015)
*Sansho the Bailiff* (*Sanshō dayu*, Mizoguchi Kenji, 1954)
*Season of the Sun* (*Taiyō no kisetsu*, Furukawa Takumi, 1956)

*Seven Samurai* (*Shichinin no samurai,* Kurosawa Akira, 1954)

*Shanghai Express* (Josef von Sternberg, 1932)

*Shozo, a Cat and Two Women, A* (*Neko to Shōzō to futari no onna,* Toyoda Shirō, 1956)

*Sisters of the Gion* (*Gion no kyōdai,* Mizoguchi Kenji, 1936)

*Snow Country* (*Yukiguni,* Toyoda Shirō, 1957)

*Snow White and Seven Dwarfs* (David Hand, Larry Morey, Wilfred Jackson, Ben Sharpsteen, Perce Pearce, William Cottrell, 1938)

*Star Wars* (George Lucas, 1977)

*Steamboat Willie* (Walt Disney and Ub Iwerks, 1928)

*Strange Tale of Oyuki, The* (*Bokutō kidan,* Toyoda Shirō, 1960)

*Take Care of My Cat* (*Goyangireul Butakhae,* Jeong Jae-eun, South Korea, 2001)

*Tale of the White Serpent, The* (*Hakujaden,* Yabushita Taiji and Ōkawa Hiroshi, 1956)

*Ten Commandments* (Cecil B. DeMille, 1956)

*That Darn Cat!* (Robert Stevenson, 1965)

*Third Man, The* (Carol Reed, 1949)

*To Catch a Thief* (Alfred Hitchcock, 1955)

*Tojuro's Love* (*Tōjurō no koi,* Yamamoto Kajirō, 1937)

*Tsuruhachi Tsurujirō* (Naruse Mikio, 1938)

*Ugetsu* (*Ugetsu monogatari,* Mizoguchi Kenji, 1953)

*Water Magician, The* (*Taki no shiraito,* Mizoguchi Kenji, 1933)

*Wild Geese, The* (*Gan,* Toyoda Shirō, 1953)

*Wolf Man, The* (George Wagner, 1941)

*Woman in the Window, The* (Fritz Lang, 1944)

*World of Susie Wong, The* (Richard Kwan, 1959)

*Yojimbo* (*Yōjimbō,* Kurosawa Akira, 1961)

An extensive list of films with cats can be found on such websites as "Cinema Cats: From Feline Film Stars to Kitty Cameos." http://www.cinemacats.com

# References

Abel, Richard, ed. 1988. *French Film Theory and Criticism: A History/Anthology 1907–1939, vol. II 1929–1939*. Princeton: Princeton University Press.

Anderson, Benedict. 1983. *Imagined Communities: Reflections on the Origins and Spread of Nationalism*. London: Verso.

Andrew, Dudley. 2009. "The Core and the Flow of Film Studies." *Critical Inquiry* 35: 879–915.

———. 1976. *The Major Film Theories: An Introduction*. Oxford: Oxford University Press.

Appadurai, Arjun. 1996. *Modernity at Large: Cultural Dimensions of Globalization*. Minneapolis: University of Minnesota Press.

Arnheim, Rudolph. 1974. *Art and Visual Perception: A Psychology of the Creative Eye*. Berkeley: University of California Press.

Astruc, Alexandre. 1968. "The Birth of a New Avant-garde: *La Caméra-Stylo*." In *The New Wave: Critical Landmarks*, edited and translated by Peter Graham, pp. 17–24. London: Secker.

Barthes, Roland. 1977. "The Death of the Author." In *Image/Music/Text*, translated and edited by Stephen Heath, pp. 142–148. London: Fontana.

Baxter, Peter. 1993. *Just Watch!: Sternberg, Paramount and America*. London: BFI.

Bazin, André. 1985. "On the *politiques des auteurs*." In *Cahiers du Cinéma: The 1950s: Neo-Realism, Hollywood, New Wave*, edited by Jim Hillier, pp. 248–259. Cambridge, MA: Harvard University Press.

———. 1960. "The Ontology of the Photographic Image." Translated by Hugh Gray. *Film Quarterly* 13(4): 4–9.

———. 2004. *What Is Cinema?* Volume 1 & 2. Translated by Hugh Gray. Berkeley: University of California Press.

Benedict, Ruth. 1989. *The Chrysanthemum and the Sword: Patterns of Japanese Culture*. Boston: Houghton Mifflin.

Bordwell, David, Janet Staiger, and Kristin Thompson. 1985. *The Classical Hollywood Cinema: Film Style and Mode of Production to 1960*. New York: Columbia University Press.

Brill, Lesley. 1988. *The Hitchcock Romance: Love and Irony in Hitchcock's Films.* Princeton, NJ: Princeton University Press.

Bugler, Caroline. 2011. *The Cat: 3500 Years of the Cat in Art.* London: Merrell.

Butler, Judith. 1990. *Gender Trouble: Feminism and the Subversion of Identity.* London: Routledge, 1990.

———, and Liz Kotz. 1992. "The Body You Want: Liz Kotz Interviews Judith Butler." *Artforum International* 31(3): 82–89.

Caughie, John, ed. 1981. *Theories of Authorship.* London: Routledge.

Chandler, Daniel. 2017. "An Introduction to Genre Theory." http://www.aber. ac.uk/media/Documents/intgenre/chandler_genre_theory.pdf. Accessed 18 July 2017.

Chopra-Gant, Mike. 2008. *Cinema and History: The Telling of Stories.* London: Wallflower.

Chow, Rey. 2001. "A Phantom Discipline." *PMLA* 116(5): 1386–1395.

"Core of the Movie: The Chase." 1995. *New York Times Magazine,* 29 October 1950: 22–23. Reprinted in *Hitchcock on Hitchcock: Selected Writings and Interviews,* edited by Sidney Gottlieb, pp. 44–46. Berkeley: University of California Press.

Davis, Darrell William. 1996. *Picturing Japaneseness: Monumental Style, National Identity, Japanese Film.* New York: Columbia University Press.

Dick, Philip K. 1968. *Do Androids Dream of Electric Sheep?* New York: Doubleday.

Dietrich, Marlene. 1961. *Marlene Dietrich's ABC.* New York: Doubleday.

Doane, Mary Ann. 1982. "Film and the Masquerade: Theorising the Female Spectator." *Screen* 23(3–4): 74–88.

Dyer, Richard. 1979. *Stars.* London: BFI.

Eisenstein, Sergei. 1998. *The Eisenstein Reader,* edited by Richard Taylor and translated by Richard Taylor and William Powell. London: BFI.

Esquevin, Christian. 2014. "Marlene Dietrich & Travis Banton." *Silver Screen Modes,* 3 February 2014. http://silverscreenmodes.com/marlene-dietrich-travis-banton/. Accessed 14 July 2017.

Evans, Kay. 1932. "Will Marlene Break the Spell?" *Photoplay* 41(3): 104.

Foucault, Michel. 1973. *The Birth of the Clinic: An Archeology of Medical Perception,* translated by Alan Sheridan. New York: Pantheon.

———. 1977. *Discipline and Punish: The Birth of the Prison,* translated by Alan Sheridan. New York: Pantheon.

———. 1984. "What Is an Author?" Translated by Josue V. Harari. In *The Foucault Reader,* edited by Paul Rainbow, pp. 101–120. New York: Pantheon.

Galt, Rosalind. 2015. "Cats and the Moving Image: Feline Cinematicity from Lumière to Maru." In *Animal Life in the Moving Image,* edited by Michael Lawrence and Laura McMahon, pp. 42–57. London: BFI.

Hansen, Miriam. 1999. "The Mass Production of the Senses: Classical Cinema as Vernacular Modernism." *Modernism/Modernity* 6(2): 59–77.

———. 2010. "Vernacular Modernism: Tracking Cinema on a Global Scale." In *World Cinemas, Transnational Perspectives,* edited by Natasa Durovicova and Kathleen Newman, pp. 287–314. New York: Routledge.

Hasumi, Shigehiko. 2008. *Eiga hōkai zenya* [The night before the cinema collapses]. Tokyo: Seido sha.

———. 1990. *Eiga yūwaku no ekurichūru* [Cinema: Writing of temptation]. Tokyo: Chikuma shobō.

Hayward, Susan. 1996. *Key Concepts in Cinema Studies*. London: Routledge.

Heath, Stephen. 1978. "Questions of Property: Film and Nationhood." *Cinetracts* 1(4): 2–11.

Higham, Charles. 1970. *Hollywood Cameraman: Sources of Light*. Bloomington: Indiana University Press.

Gottlieb, Sidney, ed. 1995. *Hitchcock on Hitchcock: Selected Writings and Interviews*. Berkeley: University of California Press.

Hyussen, Andreas. 1994. *Twilight Memories: Marking Time in a Culture of Amnesia*. London: Routledge.

Inaga, Shigemi. 2014. *Kaiga no rinkai: Kindai higashi Ajia bijutsushi no shikkoku to meiun* [*Images on the edge: A historical survey of east Asian trans-cultural modernities*]. Nagoya: Nagoya daigaku shuppankai.

———. 1997. *Kaiga no tasogare: Eduāru Mane botsugo no tōsō* [*The twilight of images: Battles after the death of Édouard Manet*]. Nagoya: Nagoya daigaku shuppankai.

Irie, Takako. 1957. *Eiga joyū* [Motion picture actress]. Tokyo: Gakufū shoin.

Iwagō, Mitsuaki. 2007. *Neko o toru* [Photographing cats]. Tokyo: Asahi shinbun sha.

Jacobs, Lea. 1993. "Belasco, DeMille, and the Development of Lasky Lighting." *Film History* 5(4): 405–418.

Kaplan, E. Ann. 1983. *Women and Film: Both Sides of the Camera*. New York: Methuen.

Kennedy, Philip. 2017. "Obsesses with Cats: The Ukiyo-e Prints of Utagawa Kuniyoshi." http://illustrationchronicles.com/Obsessed-with-Cats-The-Ukiyo-e-Prints-of-Utagawa-Kuniyoshi. Accessed 10 August 2017.

Lacan, Jacques. 1978. *Seminar XI: The Four Fundamental Concepts of Psychoanalysis*, translated by Alan Sheridan. New York: Norton.

LaMarre, Thomas. 2009. *The Anime Machine: A Media Theory of Animation*. Minneapolis: University of Minnesota Press.

———. 2002. "From Animation to *Anime*: Drawing Movements and Moving Drawings." *Japan Forum* 14(2): 329–367.

Lehman, Peter, and William Luhr. 1981. *Blake Edwards*. Athens: Ohio University Press.

Letouzé, Maurice. 1990. "La Peinture Japonaise" [The Japanese painting] in *L'Exposition et ses attractions*, Tome XVI (Paris, 1900), 49–52, quoted and translated to Japanese in Tano Yasunori, "Pari bankokuhakurankai to Nihon bijutsu" (Paris Exhibition and Japanese art). In *Nippon Bijutsuin Hyakunenshi*, 2 kan Jō (Zuhan hen) (One Hundred Year History of Nippon Bijutsuin, volume 2–1, graphics), edited by Nippon Bijutsuin Hyakunenshi Henshūshitsu, p. 445. Tokyo: Nippon bijutsuin.

Looser, Thomas. 2006. "Superflat and the Layers of Image and History in 1990s Japan." *Mechadmia* 1: 92–109.

Marcus, Laura. 2007. "Cinematic Realism: 'A recreation of the world in its own image.'" In *Adventures in Realism,* edited by Matthew Beaumont, pp. 177–192. Malden, MA: Blackwell.

Miura, Mitsuo. 1940. "Haikō" [Lighting]. In *Eiga satsueigaku dokuhon* [Cinematography reader], edited by Tane Shigeru, pp. 237–252. Tokyo: Dainihon eiga kyōkai.

Miyao, Daisuke. 2013. *The Aesthetics of Shadow: Lighting and Japanese Cinema.* Durham: Duke University Press.

———. 2002. "Before Anime: Animation and the Pure Film Movement in Prewar Japan." *Japan Forum* 14(2): 191–209.

———. 2007. *Sessue Hayakawa: Silent Cinema and Transnational Stardom.* Durham, NC: Duke University Press.

Morita Fujio. 2007. "Nihon eiga no jidaigeki saho dai 3 kai" [Methods of *jidaigeki* in Japanese cinema 3]. *Eiga Satsuei* 172: 66–79.

Mosley, Rachel. 2002. *Growing up with Audrey Hepburn: Text, Audience, Resonance.* Manchester: Manchester University Press.

Mulvey, Laura. 1999. "Visual Pleasure and Narrative Cinema." In *Film Theory and Criticism: Introductory Readings,* edited by Leo Braudy and Marshall Cohen, pp. 833–844. New York: Oxford University Press.

Murakami, Takashi. 2000. *Super Flat.* Tokyo: Madra Publishing.

Mutobe, Akinori. 2007. "Mone 'Tsumiwara' rensaku no saikō: Mochīfu, shunkansei, koten" [Rethinking Monet's series painting, *Haystacks:* Motifs, instantaneity, private exhibition]. In *Situation actuelle de l'histoire de l'art moderne francaise: Du point de vue de l'après "New Art History"* [Present situation of the history of French modern art: From the point of view after "New Art History"], edited by Nagai Takanori, pp. 163–192. Tokyo: Sangen sha.

Nakamura, Hideyuki. 2009. "In the Name of 'Film Noir'?: Reconsidering the Noir Discourse." *Iichiko: a journal for transdisciplinary studies of pratiques* 102: 69–79.

Natsume, Sōseki. 2001. *I Am a Cat,* translated by Aiko Ito and Graeme Wilson. North Clarendon, VT: Tuttle.

Neale, Steve. 1983. "Masculinity as Spectacle: Reflections on Men and Mainstream Cinema." *Screen* 24(6): 2–17.

Nitobe, Inazō. 2002. *Bushido: The Soul of Japan.* Tokyo: Kodansha International.

Newman, Kim. 1999. *Cat People.* London: BFI.

O'Brien, Charles. 1996. "Film Noir in France: Before the Liberation." *Iris* 21: 7–20.

Ōkubo, Junichi. 2008. *Karā-ban ukiyo-e* [Ukiyo-e: Color edition]. Tokyo: Iwanami shoten.

Ōtsuka, Eiji. 2003. *Atomu no meidai: Tezuka Osamu to sengo manga no shudai* [Atomu's proposition: The themes of Tezuka Osamu and postwar manga]. Tokyo: Tokuma shoten.

Raine, Michael. 2001. "Ishihara Yūjirō: Youth, Celebrity, and the Male Body in late 1950s Japan." In *Word and Image in Japanese Cinema*, edited by Dennis Washburn and Carole Cavanaugh, pp. 202–25. Cambridge: Cambridge University Press.

Rubin, James H. 2003. *Impressionist Cats and Dogs: Pets in the Painting of Modern Life*. New Haves: Yale University Press.

Said, Edward. 1979. *Orientalism*. New York: Vintage.

Saito, Ayako. 2014. "Occupation and Memory: The Representation of Woman's Body in Postwar Japanese Cinema." In *The Oxford Handbook of Japanese Cinema*, edited by Daisuke Miyao, 327–362. Oxford: Oxford University Press.

Shimizu, Isao. 2014. *Hokusai Manga: Nihon manga no genten* [Hokusai Manga: The origin of Japanese manga]. Tokyo: Heibon sha.

Shimura, Miyoko. 2001. "Onna ga neko ni naru toki: 'Kaibyō' eiga *Hiroku kaibyō den* shiron" [When a woman becomes a cat: An essay on 'Monster cat' film *The Haunted Castle*]. *Iconics: Japanese Journal of Image Arts and Sciences* 67: 41–56.

———. 2006. "Tenkanki no Tanaka Kinuyo to Irie Takako: Bakeneko to joyū no gensetsu o megutte" [Tanaka Kinuyo and Irie Takako in transitional periods: On the discourses on monster cats and actresses]. In *Eiga to shintai/sei* (Cinema and body/sex), edited by Saito Ayako, pp. 79–110. Tokyo: Shinwa sha.

Shin, Chi-Yun. 2005. "Two of a Kind: Gender and Friendship in *Friend* and *Take Care of My Cat*." In *New Korean Cinema*, edited by Chi-Yun Shin and Julian Stringer, pp. 117–131. New York: New York University Press.

Shohat, Ella, and Robert Stam. 1996. "From the Imperial Family to the Transnational Imaginary: Media Spectatorship in the Age of Globalization." In *Global/Local: Cultural Production and the Transnational Imaginary*, edited by Rob Wilson and Wimal Dissanayake, pp. 145–170. Durham, NC: Duke University Press.

Singer, Ben. 2001. *Melodrama and Modernity: Early Sensational Cinema and Its Contexts*. New York: Columbia University Press.

Sklar, Robert. 1994. *Movie-Made America: A Cultural History of American Movies*. Revised and Updated. New York: Vintage.

Souriau, Paul. 1983. *The Aesthetics of Movement*, translated and edited by Manon Souriau. Amherst: University of Massachusetts Press.

Sternberg, Josef von. 1965. *Fun in a Chinese Laundry: An Autobiography*. New York: Collier.

Studlar, Gaylyn. 1988. *In the Realm of Pleasure: Von Sternberg, Dietrich, and the Masochistic Aesthetic*. New York: Columbia University Press.

Suzuki, Junichi, and Sakakibara Rumi. 2008. *Tōyō ojisan no kamera: Shashinka Miyatake Tōyō to senjika no zaibei nikkeijin tachi* [Uncle Toyo's camera: photographer Toyo Miyatake and Japanese people in America during the war]. Tokyo: Shōgakukan.

Takahata, Isao. 1999. *Jūni seiki no animēshon: Kokuhō emakimono ni miru eiga-teki anime-teki narumono* [Animation in the twelfth century: The cinematic and animetic in national treasure scroll paintings]. Tokyo: Tokuma shoten.

Takizawa, Hajime. 1986. "Jidaigeki towa nanika" [What is *jidaigeki?*]. In *Kōza Nihon eiga 2: Musei eiga no kansei* [Lectures on Japanese cinema 2: Completion of silent cinema], edited by Imamura Shōhei, Satō Tadao, Shindō Kaneto, Tsurumi Shunsuke, and Yamada Yōji, pp. 116–131. Tokyo: Iwanami shoten.

Tanizaki, Jun'ichirō. 1982. *"Neko to Shōzō to futarino onna"* [Shozo, a Cat and Two Women]. In *Tanizaki Jun'ichirō zenshu dai 14 kan* [Complete works of Tanizaki Jun'ichiro, volume 14], pp. 263–368. Tokyo: Chūōkōron sha.

Tano, Yasunori. 1990. "Pari bankokuhakurankai to Nihon bijutsu" [Paris Exposition Universelle and Japanese art]. In *Nippon bijutsuin hyakunenshi*, 2 kan jō (zuhan hen) [One-hundred-year history of Nippon bijutsuin. Vol. 2-1 (graphics)], edited by Nippon bijutsuin hyakunenshi henshūshitsu, pp. 435–459. Tokyo: Nippon bijutsuin.

Theisen, Earl. 1934. "Part of the Story of Lighting." *International Photographer* 6(3): 10–12, 26.

Truffaut, François. 1976. "A Certain Tendency of the French Cinema." In *Movies and Methods, Vol. I,* edited by Bill Nicols, pp. 224–237. Berkeley: University of California Press.

Tsumura, Hideo. 1943. "Nihon eiga wa shinpo shitaka: Shōwa 17 nendo sakuhin kaiko" [Has Japanese cinema progressed?: Retrospective of 1942 films]. *Eiga Junpō* 71: 38–39.

Uratani, Toshiro. 2004. "Chanbara sutā retsuden" [Biographies of chanbara stars]. In *Kyōto kara sekai e: Chanbara eiga* [From Kyoto to the words: Chanbara films], edited by Yamane Sadao and Tanaka Noriko, pp. 24–27. Kyōto: Kyōto Film Festival.

Vest, James M. 2003. *Hitchcock and France: The Forging of an Auteur.* Westport, CT: Praeger.

Weiss, Andrea. 1992. *Vampires and Violets: Lesbians in the Cinema.* London: Jonathan Cape.

Yamada, Isuzu. 2000. *Eiga to tomoni* [With cinema]. Tokyo: Nihon tosho sentā.

Yamaguchi, Katsunori, and Watanabe Yasushi. 1977. *Nihon animēshon eiga shi* [The history of Japanese animation]. Osaka: Yūbun sha.

Yoshimura, Kōzaburō. 2001. *Eiga wa furēmu da!: Yoshimura Kōzaburō hito to sakuhin* [Cinema is a frame!: Yoshimura Kozaburo the person and his work]. Tokyo: Dōhō sha.

# Index

# About the Author

Daisuke Miyao is professor and Hajime Mori Chair in Japanese Language and Literature at the University of California, San Diego. Miyao is the author of *The Aesthetics of Shadow: Lighting and Japanese Cinema* and *Sessue Hayakawa: Silent Cinema and Transnational Stardom*. He also edited the *Oxford Handbook of Japanese Cinema* and coedited *Transnational Cinematography Studies* with Lindsay Coleman and Roberto Schaefer, ASC.